Restoring Righteousness

GEOFFREY
HIGHAM

Restoring Righteousness by Geoffrey Higham
Published by Creation House
A Strang Company
600 Rinehart Road
Lake Mary, Florida 32746
www.creationhouse.com

Publisher's Note: Unless otherwise noted, all Scripture quotations are the author's paraphrase. The views expressed in this book are not necessarily the views held by the publisher.

Scripture quotations marked KJV are from the King James Version of the Bible.

Scripture quotations marked NKJV are from the New King James Version of the Bible. Copyright © 1979, 1980, 1982 by Thomas Nelson, Inc., publishers. Used by permission.

Scripture quotations marked NIV are from the Holy Bible, New International Version. Copyright © 1973, 1978, 1984, International Bible Society. Used by permission.

Scripture quotations marked RSV are from the Revised Standard Version of the Bible. Copyright © 1946, 1952, 1971 by the Division of Christian Education of the National Council of the Churches of Christ in the USA. Used by permission.

Scripture quotations marked *Nestle's* are from *Nestle's Greek Text* (London: Samuel Bagster and Sons, 1984).

Definitions are from *The Concise Oxford English Dictionary* (Oxford: Oxford University Press, 2004).

Cover design by Terry Clifton

Library of Congress Control Number: 2005924887
International Standard Book Number: 1-59185-816-X

First Edition

05 06 07 08 09 — 987654321
Printed in the United States of America

They that turn many to righteousness [will shine] as the stars for ever and ever.

—DANIEL 12:3, KJV

This book is dedicated to Jesus Christ our Savior—"The Lamb of God who takes away the sin of the world" (John 1:29, NKJV). He took the punishment I deserved for my past sins and gave me His Spirit. I received a new lifestyle of freedom from further sin. Led righteously by His Spirit, I am living with the promise of eternal life in the everlasting kingdom of God. It is His promise to all who live with love for God and their neighbor.

Contents

Preface ix

Introduction 1

Part I: Reach for the Stars

1 Where Am I Heading? 5

2 Reach Up and Live 9

3 Stop Dreaming—Wake Up to Reality 11

4 The Messiah Brings Freedom 17

5 God's Goodness and His Severity 23

6 God's Grace Empowers 33

7 For Little Children, Everything Is Pure 43

8 A Reformation of Righteousness Through Love 59

9 Fear God? 71

Part II: Our Life-Changing Excursion

10 Why Did I Have to Die? 79

11 Life After Death 91

12 Bolt the Door and Windows 99

13 Don't Swallow Camels 107

14 Righteousness and Holiness! 113

15 Conditions Do Apply 119

16 Proud Humility? 125

17 What About 1 John 1:8–10? 127

18 Two Tigers 135
19 Law Is Not in the Grave! 139
20 Our Deliverance From the Law 145
21 The Law of Sin 157
22 Race to Win 173
23 Romans 8 177
24 Not Condemned—Why Not? 179
25 Am I a Christian? 189
26 Why Suffering? 197
27 Glory Awaits Us! 203

Part III: Visions, Words, and Healing

28 Visions, Words, and Dreams! 209
29 His Book and Around the World 213
30 How I Was Completely Healed of Asthma 219
31 Take Your Glory, Lord 221

Epilogue 224
Notes 225

Preface

Shall I Be Saved?

Christ says that we shall be saved by His life (Rom. 5:10). What on earth is He talking about? The word *shall* points us to a future time. It points to that day when Jesus Christ returns to either take us up with Him or send us to the everlasting fire prepared for the devil and his rebel angels. It tells us that we need to be saved in the future from being sentenced to that eternal fire, that we still need to be saved from God's wrath on that day even after we have been born again as Christians.

It tells me that I cannot have a blessed assurance of future salvation unless I have His sinless life working through me. It tells me that I have been circumcised with the circumcision not made by hands, but that my old flesh life was cut off on the cross when I was killed in crucifixion with Him (Rom. 6). It tells me that I have been fed lies which told me that because Christ's blood reconciled me to God I now have an assurance of getting into heaven. I have not! For I have to *win* the race!

The truth is that without Christ living a holy lifestyle in me, so that I am free from sinning, I cannot enter the eternal kingdom of Jesus Christ (Heb. 12:14). I was physically crucified with Jesus. Nevertheless, I physically live. Yet it is not I that physically lives but Christ who lives in me by His Spirit. And my lifestyle is His lifestyle because I now live by faith in Him, the Son of God, who loved me and gave His physical life for me (Gal. 2:20–21).

My future salvation depends entirely on my lifestyle being one of absolute obedience to the leading of the Holy Spirit who is the Spirit of Christ and the Spirit of my Father and His Father. I am in the salvation race, and unless I run according to the rules shown me by the Spirit of God I will face disqualification on the day of judgment of our works by Jesus Christ.

This is truth and we had better believe it and act on it. Tell all the pastors, even though they do not believe it! Tell your neighbors, even if it shocks them!

Dear Reader, you are my neighbor. Whatever your name, race, religion, or politics; whether we are at war or have been at war, I love you. Because I love you I want you to be happy on earth, and I want you to get to heaven. That is why I have written this book to you. Even if you are my enemy, I love you.

I love you because thirty years ago when I was under the sentence of death from my doctor I called out to God. He responded by curing me and giving me the gift of His Spirit from on high. His Spirit poured an unquenchable love into my heart which compels me to love our God with all of my being and to love you, my neighbor, as myself. When I called out to God, I did so in the name of Jesus Christ. The Holy Spirit of God has directed my life for many years now, and in this book you will discover what He has shown me about true happiness and the way to eternal life in heaven. He has asked me to share it with you. Read it with childlike faith, for without faith it is impossible to please God. May you be filled with joy forever!

You are about to experience a move of the Holy Spirit, which follows the ministry of my book, *Go and Sin No More: How to Walk in Holiness and See God.* This book expands on the doctrine of righteousness. You will learn how Romans, chapters 6–8, are at the core of Christ's gospel of life.

As far as I can ascertain, no other author has ever uncompromisingly agreed with God's prophets and with His Son Jesus and His apostles on the ministry of the Messiah to set people free from sinning. Christ empowers us to live righteously and thereby obtain an inheritance of eternal life. I am confident that these Spirit-led writings will fan a holy and worldwide church reformation. It will happen at the beginnings of our twenty-first century. Righteousness will be restored!

We are preparing the way for the return of our Messiah and His kingdom.

You are about to dine on a truly satisfying meal of scriptures. To whet your appetite, I offer you these few nibbles straight from a hot oven. Some may taste bitter, but in your stomach they will become as sweet as honey.

Daniel prophesied that when Messiah comes, He will:

> ...finish the transgression, and...make an end of sins, and...make reconciliation for iniquity, and...bring in everlasting *righteousness*...
>
> —Daniel 9:24

Zacharias, John's father, prophesied in Luke 1:74–75 that we, "being delivered out of the hand of our enemies," could serve

God without fearfulness in holiness and righteousness all the days of our lives. Jesus, the Messiah Himself, said that whoever commits sin is a slave of sin. However, if the Son makes us free from that slave master, we "shall be free indeed" (John 8:36).

Paul the Apostle stated in Romans 8:2 that the unwritten law of the Spirit of life in Christ Jesus has set us free from the unwritten law of sin and death. Take a look at 1 John 3:6–10. Also, the apostle Peter emphatically declares in 1 Peter 4:2 that because the Messiah came, we should no longer live according to the lusts of our flesh but according to the will of God.

Maybe, just maybe, our failure to grasp what the Messiah has promised is the reason the church has lived such a fragmented and torrid life for two thousand years and now appears, in some quarters, to be going mad.

Bon appetit!

Introduction

Treat this book as an adventure. Before we begin, I invite you to join me in saying this prayer aloud:

> *Dear Jesus, take my heart. Shake it, break it, and remake it until it is one with Yours. Cleanse me of any stubborn mind-sets. Open my eyes afresh to the truths of Your Father's words and promises to me. Show me if there is deception in my foundations. May this day be the start of a beautiful lifestyle of love and righteousness, with freedom from sin. I believe Your promise that each day You will keep me blameless through Your power of love and my faith. Thank You for Your gift of grace from Your Spirit. May I truly be freed to reach for the stars and serve You in Your purpose for my life. Holy Spirit, put Your arm around*

me, and fill this earthen jar with Your sweet wine of love. Draw me closer to You. I want to be a worthy friend, a spotless bride, an ambassador of the King, Your Majesty. I am longing to see You forever. Amen.

Part I:

Reach for the Stars

Chapter 1

Where Am I Heading?

At the end of my days, one of two destinations awaits me. I either go to eternal life with God in heaven or to eternal death with Satan in the lake of fire.

A master of Scripture asked Jesus publicly, "What shall I do to inherit eternal life?" Jesus answered, "What do you believe the Law says?" He answered, "You shall love the Lord your God with all your heart, and with all your soul, and with all your strength, and with all your mind and your neighbor as yourself." Jesus replied, "Your answer is correct. Do it and you shall have life [eternal]" (Luke 10:25–28). Our eternal inheritance, therefore, is dependent on our righteous lifestyle of deeds of love toward God and man. But you say, "Where does faith come into it?" Here is the answer: without faith in Jesus

Christ and His promises, it is impossible to walk in a righteous lifestyle of works of love toward God and man (Gal. 2:21). But you will say, "Where does grace come in?" The answer is that we are indebted to God's grace both for our day-by-day faith and our day-by-day righteous life of good works of love (Eph. 2:7–10). The man who asked Jesus about eternal life after death had the right answer but He did not have the means to do it for he was still in the Law covenant (Gal. 3:11). Therefore, Jesus had to come down from heaven as God in flesh to establish a new covenant in His own blood (1 Cor. 11:25). Paul sums it up in his letter to the church in Galatia: "If you are justified by the Law, Christ has become of no use to you and you have fallen from God's grace. For we wait for the hope of eternal life by our righteous works of love which flow out to us from our trust in Christ" (Gal. 5:4–5). It is His Spirit who brings this love to us, therefore we wait for our inheritance with confidence. For whether you are under the Law or not under the Law it is of no benefit. There is only one thing that will allow you to get your inheritance and that is faith in Jesus Christ working through love (Gal. 5:6).

The apostle John gives confirmation to Paul for he declares that we have to *do* righteously to be righteous and that by abiding in faith in Christ we do not sin (1 John 3:6–7). The gospel of Jesus Christ may therefore be defined as faith in Jesus Christ, which produces righteous works of love that guarantee us eternal life after death. For the righteous fulfillment of God's laws is in loving your neighbor as yourself (Gal. 5:14). It is only part of the truth to believe that we are saved from God's wrath by grace alone. Grace is the vehicle that brings us the power to love God and man, and it is for a purpose. This book will show you scripturally how to grasp that purpose. His grace comes to us by the Spirit of grace (Heb. 10:29). That Spirit is the Spirit of Christ Jesus Himself (Rom 8:9).

However, Jesus and the lawyer both knew it was impossible at that time for any man to fulfil the righteousness of the Law by loving God and his neighbor in this way. As Romans 3:23 says, "For all have sinned." And 1 John 1:10 adds, "If we say that we have not sinned, we make [God] a liar, and his word is not in us." Jesus had yet to make a way by which mankind could live a righteous lifestyle of obedience to God's will and truly love Him and his fellow man, even when that man is an enemy.

This book is written to clear away all religious and nonreligious misconceptions of how to obtain eternal life. It will show you how to be certain of eternal life, which is God's reward for doing His works of loving God and our fellow man. I must cease from my own works of righteousness and do God's. In the words of 1 John 2:29, "If ye know that he is righteous, ye know that every one that doeth righteousness is born of [God]."

This book will help keep us from what the Bible, in Revelation 20:14, calls the second death—being sent in shame to be eternally entombed with Satan in the lake of fire.

> ...the mercy of the LORD is from everlasting to everlasting upon them that fear him, and his righteousness unto children's children.
>
> —PSALM 103:17

Chapter 2

Reach Up and Live

Jesus Christ graciously filled me with His Spirit when I was forty-eight. The first words that came out of my mouth were "reach for the stars." God has already reached down from the heavens to earth. He sent His Son down with His love to redeem the world from sin. Because of my belief in Christ and His promises and my hunger for the Holy Spirit, He reached down and baptized me in His love. I was filled with the Spirit of God, who brings His grace to mankind.

Reaching for the stars, I have found, is a call to respond to His redeeming love and grace by spiritually reaching up with an open heart and mind to receive the lifestyle of the high calling of God. It is responding with body, soul, and spirit. It is a continual reaching up in praise, love, and thanksgiving to our merciful and loving Father, "Who hath delivered us from the power of darkness, and hath translated us into the kingdom of his dear Son" (Col. 1:13). Reaching for the stars is seeking those things that are above, "where Christ sitteth on the right hand" of our Father (Col. 3:1). It means aiming for the best!

> Blessed are they that keep judgment, and he that doeth righteousness at all times.
>
> —Psalm 106:3

Chapter 3

STOP DREAMING—WAKE UP TO REALITY

CHARLES SPURGEON GIVES this warning:

> *Christian*, beware how thou thinkest lightly of sin. Take heed lest thou fall little by little. Sin, a little thing? Is it not a poison? Who knows its deadliness? Sin a little thing? Do not little foxes ruin the grapes? Doth not the tiny coral polyp build a reef that wrecks a navy? Do not little strokes fell lofty oak trees? Will not continual droppings wear away stones? Sin a little thing? It girded the Redeemer's head with thorns, and pierced His heart! It made him suffer anguish, bitterness and woe. Could we weigh the least sin in the scales of eternity, we would fly from it as from a serpent, and abhor the least appearance of evil. Look on all sin as that which

> crucified the Savior, and you will find it to be exceedingly sinful.[1]

What does our risen Lord think of sin?

Less than fifty years after Jesus of Nazareth ascended back to heaven, He spoke from behind the apostle John on the Greek island of Patmos. He startled him with the words: "I am Alpha and Omega, the first and the last. I am He who liveth, and was dead. I am alive for evermore, and have the keys of hell and of death. Write what I show you to the seven churches which are in Asia" (Rev. 1:11, 18).

Christ's messages through John show that God assesses His people like all people—on their works. "Jesus Christ is the same yesterday, today, and forever" (Hebrews 13:8, NKJV). Therefore it should be bold-type, front-page, daily news in every church that, as Jesus told John, only those who overcome temptation and sin shall not be punished by the second death.

The purpose of this book is to show born-of-the-Spirit Christians and others the way to overcome temptation and sin. The words of Jesus to the church at Smyrna, found in Revelation 2:8–11, leave no room for doubt that we must overcome sin in this life if we are to have eternal life and avoid eternal fire in the next!

This book is a message of scriptural warning for the twenty-first-century church to wake up from the opium-like dream of a peaceful assurance of future salvation and inheritance. It is a call to live the "kingdom life." It is time to stop sinning, church, and to return to reality before it is too late (Rev. 2:11; 20:14).

Christ's message to the church at Sardis is even more pungent than the one to Smyrna: "Only a few of the entire church have not defiled their garments [with sinning], and they only shall walk with me in white; for they alone are worthy" (Rev. 3:4). At their conversion the people in the Sardis church had all been given white, spotless garments washed by His blood. But since then, their willful sinning had spattered their freshly washed robes with unacceptable dirt. Jesus continues:

> He that overcometh, the same shall be clothed in white raiment; and I will not blot out his name out of the book of life, but I will confess his name before my Father, and before his angels.
>
> —Revelation 3:5

We know that we are reconciled to God by His grace—simply by trusting in Christ's death—and not by our own good works. But after reconciliation, Jesus warns us that we can be sure of avoiding the second death only by a continuing sinless lifestyle in Him. Romans 5:10 says that "being reconciled, we shall be saved by his life." Only the overcomers are assured of being worthy of their heavenly inheritance.

The time for using Christianity as some sort of self-assuring, flesh-satisfying drug is past. Some in the younger generation have found better drugs in chemicals to lull them into a state of peaceful self-assurance that, for a time, all is well. The wide road to destruction is packed with souls, and many of them are Christians who have been deceived. In affluent countries, the churches are seeing a great falling-away of their followers. The Holy Spirit is shouting that time is up!

Thank God, the Christian has hope and power and potential that comes from beyond himself. In the following chapters, we will learn the way back.

God has provided a key that will lock every door and window against the entry of sin. That key is Jesus Christ, His only begotten Son. We place the key in the lock by our faith, which He gives us as a gift.

Recently I read a book about our victory over sin and sinning. The author ruined it by contradicting himself and saying that we will sin in spite of Christ. Yet, nowhere in the New

Testament do we find a writer declaring that a walking-in-the-Spirit Christian will sin. A man with measles will be covered with spots, but as soon the disease is finished, the spots disappear. If we know that our disease of sin is finished, our sinning disappears. Too easy!

Imagine that you are sitting at the beginning of the runway in a plane that has been built by God, and the pilot is Jesus Christ Himself. Your faith might be small, but at this moment it is big. You are positive that with Christ at the controls, you are going to reach your destination safely. For once, you do not have any thought that the plane might crash. You are fully relaxed. You sense the angels at the wing tips and the Holy Spirit as He navigates.

But suddenly, just as you are expecting to hear the engines roar to life, a voice on the intercom says: "This aircraft is built by almighty God, and your captain is His Son, Jesus Christ. However, we need to advise you to carry out the following safety instructions if we crash—as one day we certainly will!"

What a shock! You are plunged into utter confusion, especially since you believe you have just heard the voice of the Captain, or at least His approved second officer. Actually, the message came from Satan. The Captain allowed him to speak through the second officer so that your faith would be tested. When you hear that same message in church, rejoice, for the testing of your faith leads to patience and perfection (James 1:3–4).

Walking-in-the-Spirit Christians are in that perfect, God-made and God-flown airplane. However, deliberate sinning will cause the floor to open beneath us and result in our fall to spiritual death, as described in Hebrews 10:26–31.

Doubt opens the door of our inner man to sin and sinning. It is, of course, wishful thinking to imagine that sinning cannot eject us from your blessed assurance in Christ. But we are not speaking about wishful thinking; we are talking about twisting the truth. The New Testament clearly teaches that we are free from sin and sinning in Christ Jesus. Yet, we are mostly taught—and wrongly so—that in spite of all Christ has promised, we will certainly sin.

Do these teachers realize that just one sin gouges out the eye of the One they say is their Savior, their heavenly bridegroom, their best friend, their Lord and their God? That only one sin can keep me out of heaven, Christian or not? That just one sin would have required the sacrifice of God's Son on that cross of torture and death? If the life of Christ within me is not good enough to keep me sinless, Christ wasted His time coming to earth and suffering a horrible death. That's Bible!

> Riches profit not in the day of wrath: but righteousness delivereth from death.
>
> —Proverbs 11:4

Chapter 4

The Messiah Brings Freedom

DANIEL, A LEADING prophet of Israel, prophesied in Daniel 9:24 that when the Messiah came, there would be reconciliation and no more transgressions or sins. Jesus Christ has fulfilled Daniel's prophecy. As 1 John 3:4 says, transgressions are the overt sins against the written Law. And in Matthew 5:27–32, we see that sins are all the other ways we can defy God's will in thought word or deed. This reconciliation is the once-and-for-all reconciliation to God by Christ's blood.

Paul taught by way of revelation from Christ that the very cause of transgressions—the written Law—because of weak flesh, was replaced by the living law of the Spirit. The written Law is not dead, but, as Romans 7:4 says, we are dead to the Law. Even the removal of written laws should not have been a surprise to the Jews. The prophet Jeremiah, speaking by the Holy Spirit, had foretold, "But this shall be the covenant that I will make with the house of Israel; After those days, saith the Lord, I will put my law in their inward parts, and write it in their hearts" (Jer. 31:33).

It is a stumbling block to the Jews if we Christians do not lay claim to the Messiah's promise that we are freed from all sinning in Jesus Christ (John 8:34, 36; 1 John 3:9). How can we expect a Jew to accept a Messiah who does not fulfil Daniel's prophecy concerning His power over further sinning?

The whistle has blown! The time is up, church, and we must accept the truth and tell it to the Jews and the world: as Romans 6:11 declares, we are dead to sin and alive to God in the Messiah, Christ Jesus.

You may have been taught that the Christian walk is one of making correct moral choices—choosing to do the right thing in every situation that arises each day. But that is not God's way. It is incorrect teaching. His command is simply to be obedient to the direction of the Holy Spirit in everything. A Christian is required by God to make only *one* choice—choose whom you will serve. From then on, it is obedience!

Romans 8:14 says that in obeying the leading of the Holy Spirit, we are sons of God. Also, 1 Samuel 15:22, says, "To obey is better than sacrifice." Only obedient sons are in line for an inheritance. According to Hebrews 9:15, the inheritance promised to sons is *eternal life* in heaven (1 Pet. 1:9; 2 Pet. 1:10–11).

Flesh-controlled people want to make choices because choosing keeps them in control of their situations and allows them to avoid obedience. Soldiers who make their own choices risk being shot by their commander! They are potential rebels. But Romans 7:19 says that when they want to choose right, they do wrong instead.

Eve, the first woman, made her own moral choice. Instead of being obedient, she fell and committed the sin of imbibing in that which God had forbidden—the knowledge of good and evil. Simple obedience would have kept her sinless and unpunished. Christian women are still required to simply obey their own husband.

The scene in the Garden of Eden (Gen. 3) is a revelation of God's unchanging plan and command for His people who are called by His Name to acknowledge Him as King. It is a very simple command: obey Him (Rom. 6:16; 1 Sam. 15:22)!

The leading of God's Holy Spirit comes to us through our faith! In Romans 1:16-17 and 8:2 we find that through faith in Christ and His promise, the law of the Spirit of life in Him has set us free from the control of the law of sin. By our faith in Christ and His promises, we are directed by His Spirit. As Galatians 2:20 teaches, it is no longer I who lives, but Christ who lives in me! We cast away our fallible decision-making process, and we accept by faith the infallible decisions of the indwelling Spirit of Christ Jesus (Rom. 8:4).

Acts 1:5 and 8 speak of the promise of the Holy Spirit and the power of God He gives. In 1 Peter 1:5, the apostle Peter says that we are kept (righteous and holy) by the power of God. Many shallow teachers contradict Scripture and say that Christians do not need to be kept.

Peter explains in 1 Peter 1:4 that this Holy Spirit power is what gives us the living hope of an incorruptible and undefiled inheritance that does not fade away. Christ received His inheritance promised to Him by His Father, and we too are recipients of the same promise. We are certain to receive it if we persevere to the end. We, like Jesus, will enjoy it eternally in resurrected, spiritual bodies—not flesh and blood bodies (1 Cor. 15:50).

First Peter 1:5 confirms Paul's teaching about our future inheritance by stating that we are kept righteous and holy "by the power of God through faith unto salvation," which is ready to be revealed in the last day.

Paul says that God's Spirit keeps us holy and righteous so

that at the reappearing of Christ Jesus, we will be able to be eternally saved (2 Pet. 1:11). He is talking about our judgment by Christ, a judgment of where Christians will spend eternity, not our position in heaven. He teaches that the end purpose of our faith is the salvation of our soul.

Our eternal salvation is not assured unless we hear those words "Well *done,* good and faithful servant" at Christ's return (Matt 25:23). On that day, as 1 Peter 1:17 says, we will be judged according to our works! He exhorts us to be holy as obedient children, because it is written:

> Be ye holy as I am holy and if you call on the Father who judges *not on who you are* but according to your works, pass your time on earth in fear; remembering that you were bought back from being under the control of sin not by mere gold or silver but by Christ's precious blood [His life].
>
> —1 PETER 1:16–19

Hebrews 10:26–29 explains that through deliberate sin or consistent sinning, a Christian—who has tasted walking in the Spirit—counts the blood of the covenant "an unholy thing" and insults the Holy Spirit of grace.

Only God can keep us faultless. Jude 24, speaking of the absolutely essential need to be kept holy and blameless all our life, says, "Now unto him that is able to keep you from falling, and to present you faultless before the presence of his glory with exceeding joy." We need to be kept holy, and therefore we need to be sure that we do not die in our sins. Who of us knows when our hour of death will come? As Jesus revealed in Mark 8:36, "...what shall it profit a man, if he shall gain the whole world, and lose his own soul?" Here, Jesus was speaking to the God-chosen people of His day. We are the God-chosen people of our day. Take heed!

Notice that Jude does not say, "...who is able to present

you by your regular repentance and His forgiveness nor by the atonement," but by being kept from falling and thereby living a faultless lifestyle, ready to meet our judge at any instant. It is by His keeping power and our subsequently blameless lifestyle that we come before His presence for all eternity. It is termed eternal life! First John 3:7 says that it is the one who *does* righteously who is righteous. We Christians should know as our first principle that, according to Hebrews 12:14, no man can see God without a holy lifestyle.

> Zion shall be redeemed with judgment, and her converts with righteousness. And the destruction of the transgressors and of the sinners [shall be] together…
>
> —Isaiah 1:27–28

Chapter 5

God's Goodness and His Severity

It is, I believe, self-evident from Scripture that we are reconciled to God through Christ's blood by faith alone. *Reconciliation* is sometimes referred to as "deliverance" or even "salvation," and therefore, it is important that we do not confuse our initial deliverance (salvation and reconciliation) with our future eternal salvation. How could our past lifestyle of sinful works ever hope to qualify us for reconciliation? It would be impossible, for, as Romans 3:23 says, "All have sinned, and come short of the glory of God."

My dear reader, Christ came to provide forgiveness for our past sins (Rom. 3:25) and to empower us to have a blameless, righteous, and holy lifestyle after our reconciliation. It is your reconciliation to God that is by faith alone. From then on, it is by our faith working through love. It is about faith and our works of love. First John 3:8 says that Jesus, Lord of heaven and earth, came to destroy the works of the devil (Rom. 5:10; Gal. 5:6)!

Hebrews 4:12–13 explains that the Christian life is open before God. It is not, as is sometimes taught, hidden from God's sight. Our own selfish will is hidden—dead and gone—if we are in Christ, according to Colossians 3:3. As Galatians 2:20 says, it is no longer I who live, but Christ who lives in me. But our lifestyle, whether it is in or out of Christ, is open and cannot be hidden before Him (Psalm 139:1–6).

When God's people were in Egypt, His destroyer passed over the houses where blood could be seen on the doorposts. God knew of all their sinning. The blood did not hide their sins, but it protected them from God's wrath, which was due to them. They were guilty but delivered by the mercy of their "Pharaoh" in heaven! The blood does not protect anyone from Satan. It protects them from God's righteous wrath toward sin.

Later, after they had been delivered from bondage to the Egyptians, God's people foolishly thought that in the freedom of the wilderness they were still under the original blood covering. Imagining that God would not see them from inside His dark cloud on the mountaintop, they openly sinned. Exodus 32 tells how they formed handmade gods and worshipped them. We are called by God not to follow their foolish and presumptuous ways. God holds His own people more accountable than He does unbelievers. Colossians 3:5 warns that our covetousness is idolatry.

In the Garden of Eden, Satan persuaded Eve that God would not cause her to die if she ate of the forbidden fruit of the tree of the knowledge of good and evil. Eve was an easy target because she knew that God was her loving Father and, I believe, foolishly thought He would never hurt her because she was His beloved daughter. And anyway, she probably thought He is not around to see my disobedient action.

But God did see, and God does keep to His promises. Genesis 3 tells how Eve suffered immediate spiritual death and was expelled from paradise. Her weak husband fared no better.

In the light of these God-given examples of the ease with which His people act presumptuously and foolishly, it is a *satanic misinterpretation of Scripture* to teach that our sinning is hidden from God because we claim to be in Christ. It will lead to spiritual death. The atonement always has been and always will be *only* for sins committed in *ignorance.* That is from the Bible as shown in Hebrews 9:7 and 10:26–31 in the New King James Version and in *Nestle's Greek Text.*

Since the days of the sixteenth century, when the church underwent a reformation-cum-rebellion, it has been widely accepted that being delivered at one's conversion unalterably guarantees the assurance of one's eternal salvation. No conditions apply! It was, I believe, an overreaction to the errors of the day.

This teaching is supported by isolated and what appear to be favorable scriptures, and it soon led to the ridiculous teaching that people who are saints are sinners at the same time. To declare that saints can be sinners at the same time is ridiculous. It is a contradiction of terms in the science of logic and, indeed, a contradiction of common sense. Believers are not expected by God to be gullible and foolish, but to rightly divide the Word of truth. It is obvious from the Bible that God, like Paul, does not tolerate fools.

It is true that if a Spirit-filled believer walks continuously by faith in the law of the Spirit of life in Christ Jesus, he cannot be condemned. However, the New Testament writers always include in each of their letters a section which severely warns Christians that eternal salvation can easily be lost forever through carelessness and willful sinning. Romans 11:22 teaches that God's goodness must always be weighted alongside God's severity.

Hebrews 9:12 is a well-used, yet isolated verse which newly

born-of-the-Spirit believers are taught. It speaks about Christ's blood having obtained eternal redemption. This can be interpreted to mean that our redemption (deliverance) is eternally secured, or that redemption is available forever by one sacrifice.

The correct meaning of this verse is clarified by continuing to read the same letter for another forty-one verses. In Hebrews 10:26–29, the writer states unambiguously that if a born-of-the-Spirit Christian sins willfully, "there remaineth no more sacrifice for sins, But a certain fearful looking for of judgment and fiery indignation," which devours sinners. Therefore, the teaching *once saved, always saved* is subject to conditions. Otherwise, it can promote carelessness, which in turn leads to willful sinning. This insults the Spirit of grace and is the unforgivable sin. Sinning turns grace into disgrace.

Peter's second letter unquestionably teaches that a Christian has to be sharp and on guard against losing his future eternal salvation. He writes: "For if after they have escaped the pollutions of the world through the knowledge of the Lord and Saviour Jesus Christ, they are again entangled therein, and overcome, the latter end is worse with them than the beginning" (2 Pet. 2:20). He continues in chapter 3 and says that a Christian rightly looks forward to new heavens and a new earth and should therefore "be diligent that ye may be found of him in peace, *without spot, and blameless*" (2 Pet. 3:13–14).

I was a "front-seat" churchgoer from childhood until the age of forty-eight. But when the Holy Spirit fell on me, I felt like I had been a bottle of dirty water that was emptied out, well-rinsed, and refilled with sweet wine. I was corked so that the wine would not become sour, contaminated, and unfit for use. Satan does not stop trying to tempt me into loosening that cork. He wants to get back in and reinfect me with the disease of sin. But I keep my cork tight by the strongest force in the universe—active faith.

Since "the righteous [will] scarcely be saved" at the judgment (1 Pet. 4:18), it would be a grave deception not to warn Christians that the race they started at conversion is full of deadly obstacles (Heb. 12:1). This race is not against others. It is against the obstacles that come from the world, the flesh, and the devil.

If we do not successfully overcome each obstacle, we risk being disqualified for life, according to Hebrews 12:17. Psalm 139:1–6 explains that almighty God sees our every move, and He judges the runners in the obstacle race. Little wonder that Philippians 2:12 teaches us to "work out your own salvation with fear and trembling."

I was permitted to enter this life-and-death race because I was set free from the power of sin at my spiritual rebirth. I became empowered by the Spirit of Jesus Christ to be an overcomer of every obstacle, according to Romans 8:2 and 4.

In this race, our judge is also our coach. It is only by faith and obedience to Him that we safely overcome every obstacle to win the prize of eternal life. Titus 3:7, 1 Corinthians 9:24, and 2 Timothy 4:7–8 describe this race. I do not write these things to shame you, but to warn you.

My dear reader, you may be thinking that even Paul was a sinner. Yes, he considered himself the greatest, but according to 1 Timothy 1:13 and 15, that was *before his conversion.* In Romans 8:2, he says that "the law of the Spirit of life in Christ Jesus hath made me free from the law of sin." Paul clearly states in 1 Corinthians 5:11 and 13 that after conversion we are not even to keep company or eat with Christians who are sinners. Put them away, he teaches us. Yet, we are not to stop loving them as brothers.

Therefore, it is clear that Paul was once a great sinner who, after conversion, became righteous. In 1 Timothy 1:16, he testifies that his life is a pattern for all sinners who become converted, born-of-the-Spirit believers. Paul's voice in Romans 6:2 echoes down through the church age: "How shall we, that are dead to sin, live any longer therein?" Paul considered himself a robber when he lawfully accepted money from a church other than the one where he was ministering. Unfortunately, some people are either unable to interpret written English properly, or they have a fixation against Paul and so teach that he was a scoundrel and a thief. They read Scripture to their own destruction.

Do Christians have temptations? Yes! Sinning? No!

It is generally accepted that the Christian church is now divided into about five hundred different denominations. I am certain, however, that they are generally united on one point of unwritten doctrine—that we will continue sinning until death.

If you know of a denomination that disagrees, please write to me. I have searched the Scriptures for thirty years and have not found a single verse that implies Christians are normally sinners. The Bible never says *when* you sin, but *if* you sin, as 1 John 2:1 illustrates. There is a world of difference in the two meanings.

If Christians find that they are still sinning, it means one of two things. Either Christ's mission to earth was a failure, or it was successful but not accepted.

Prayerfully read the following scriptures and ask yourself what they teach:

> And ye know that he was manifested to take away our sins; and in him is no sin. Whosoever abideth in him sinneth not: whosoever sinneth hath not seen him, neither known him. Little children, let no man deceive you: he that doeth righteousness is righteous, even as he is righteous. He that committeth sin is of the devil; for the devil sinneth from the beginning. For this purpose the Son of God was manifested, that he might destroy the works of the devil. Whosoever is born of God doth not commit sin; for his seed remaineth in him: and he cannot sin, because he is born of God. In this the children

> of God are manifest, and the children of the devil: whosoever doeth not righteousness is not of God, neither he that loveth not his brother.
>
> —1 JOHN 3:5–10

Sadly, especially since the time of the Reformation in the sixteenth century, the church has painted itself into a corner and has no way out but to flatly deny the original meaning of certain New Testament scriptures. Are we saying that Christ failed or that we will not accept His victory?

John 1:12 states that God gives all who accept (receive) Christ the power to become His sons. In Romans 8:14, Paul explains that this power is the Spirit of Jesus Christ, for it is in obeying the leading the Holy Spirit that we qualify to be the sons of God.

Consider the promise of Jesus, our blessed Savior:

> Verily, verily, I say unto you, Whosoever committeth sin is the servant of sin...If the Son therefore shall make you free, ye shall be free indeed.
>
> —JOHN 8:34, 36

The apostle John certainly meant what he said in declaring that the whole purpose for Christ's first coming was to destroy the works of the devil, namely sinning. Jesus nowhere teaches that we are to avoid the temptations of the world, the flesh, or the devil. No, He simply states that He has set us free from committing sin no matter where we may go and whatever temptations may come our way.

Fleeing the occasions of sin in order to avoid sinning is not the way of Christ and His empowering Spirit; it is the way of fear and law. Is not God's grace sufficient? Jesus said that we should be in the world but not of it. False teachings are the only thing He tells us to flee!

Teresa of Avila said:

> That it would be a strange belief that when God has willed that a toad should fly, He should stand aside and wait for it to do so by its own efforts.[1]

She likened her pre-conversion life to that of a toad, inferring that if toads could fly by their own efforts, sinners could likewise escape sin by such things as contriving how to avoid the occasions of sin. All self-effort ends in failure, and that is why Jesus left His place in glory. He came to die and take us to death so that His life could become our life. In John 15:5, Jesus said that without Him we can do nothing!

Jesus is coming back a second time for a spotless bride—Christians who have lived a blameless lifestyle. By transposing a Greek sentence structure to make some real sense, we find the writer of Hebrews saying, "... unto them without sin shall He appear a second time unto salvation" (Heb. 9:28). Christians have their past sins forgiven and are empowered to continue in a righteous lifestyle. This is God's provision so that we may be saved eternally from God's wrath, when Christ judges us at His return in the clouds.

To be saved on that day, we need to be free from condemnation. The only way we can be free from condemnation is to have been set free from sin and sinning by the law of the Spirit of life in Christ Jesus. We do this by believing and confessing the promises of Romans 8:1–2 and Galatians 5:6, for nothing avails but faith working through love. The power to operate in faith and love come through a gift of God. It is by His grace.

Repentance is a hard thing because it means admitting that we were wrong. In Peter's sermon to the Jews on the Day of Pentecost, he told them to repent. It meant that they would have to admit that their pet doctrines concerning the Messiah were wrong. They would have to admit that they actually killed Him as a criminal.

Peter loved his fellow Jews too much to not put himself at grave risk by telling them the cold, hard truth. I follow in

Peter's footsteps. I love the brethren too much to refrain from asking them to repent of their mistaken belief that we can be saints and at the same time continually sinning.

My punishment is that churches tolerate me, but many do not accept me. However, they are not rejecting me, but their Savior. He died to fulfill His promise to take us to death so that:

> ...the body of sin might be destroyed, that henceforth we should not serve sin. For he that is dead is freed from sin...But God be thanked, that ye *were* the servants of sin, but ye have obeyed from the heart that form of doctrine which was delivered you...Being then made free from sin, ye became the servants of righteousness...*But now being made free from sin,* and become servants to God, ye have your fruit unto holiness, *and the end everlasting life.*
>
> —Romans 6:6–7, 17–18, 22

Our inheritance is eternal life, which is awarded to winners at the end of the race, not at the beginning. We have cheapened and reduced the salvation message into simply saying certain phrases and then being told that we are eternally saved. We have not warned about the pitfalls that lie ahead and the sins that can so easily beset us and disqualify us.

Is it any wonder that I have heard that Billy Graham is appalled at how few new Christians successfully persevere? We have sold Christ short by telling them that they will be sinners till they die but not to worry about it. We instruct them to repent every day, and this is not Christ's gospel. It is the gospel of mankind, who walk by sight rather than faith. Christ's gospel is "from faith to faith" (Rom. 1:16–17). Paul speaks in Romans 5:10 of our coming to Christ as being reconciled to God, but he insists that our future salvation is dependent on Christ's life working through us.

The salvation message is only complete when we understand, believe, and confess according to Galatians 2:20–21 that it is no longer we who live, for we have been crucified and buried. Now it is Christ who lives in us, to give us His righteous lifestyle. We should know that righteousness can come to us in no other way.

If we look to written laws for righteousness, Christ's death was pure vanity—a waste of time and effort. Galatians 2:16–19 teaches that if we are walking as we should (by faith that it is Jesus who is living our life) and yet find ourselves sinning, we have gone back to walking in the written Law and have fallen from grace.

Therefore, the reality is that we are calling Christ a sinner if we as dutiful Christians confess that we are still sinning. The Jews and the world are not impressed with our attempts at humility in confessing that our ongoing sinning is continually forgiven by an "ineffective" Messiah. They can, on the other hand, draw the valid conclusion that because of my sinning, Jesus Christ cannot be the true Messiah nor a Savior worth following. But Christ is our Messiah and He has saved us from sin and sinning!

Christians, please heed 1 Corinthians 15:3–4 and awake to reality. Our sinning brings disgrace to the name of our blessed Savior and will kill us spiritually. The Holy Spirit is our guarantee that one day we will receive our inheritance. But we can quench the Holy Spirit by insulting Him with our sinning. The word *quench* means "to put out or extinguish flames."

What I am teaching was "par for the course" in the early church and anyone acquainted with the teachings of John Wesley, the great English Revivalist of the eighteenth century, will know that he espoused what I am teaching throughout this book.[2] Hudson Taylor embraced it, and his biographers, Dr. and Mrs. Howard Taylor, highlight this fact in their book, *The Exchanged Life.*[3] We exchange our own life for Christ's!

> ...when thy judgments are in the earth, the inhabitants of the world will learn righteousness.
>
> —Isaiah 26:9

Chapter 6

God's Grace Empowers

Since we are to be judged on our works, the teaching that we are not saved by works needs to be narrowed down to the time preceding our initial deliverance (salvation). This is the deliverance that allows us to start the race. However, the race ends with meeting our judge.

I once saw a man make a wonderful start and go on to win a sailing race by defeating a hundred other boats; but his name did not appear in the list of finishers. The judges had disqualified him for breaking the rules. We Spirit-filled Christians are in a race in which we can be disqualified. If we are to judge angels, we need to have walked righteously on this earth. Church leaders will be required to overcome enormous pride to admit it.

I believe that we often misrepresent Christ's gospel when we lead past sinners to Him. If our methods were taken to a court of law, I am sure that we would be liable to charges of fraud or misrepresentation and rightly convicted for not telling the full story. Obedience to God's grace empowers us to keep within His righteous will; why are we ashamed to tell this to the new convert? Is it because we follow the teaching of men, perhaps fearing what man can do to us rather than God?

Jesus was thrown out of the synagogue, and they tried to hurl Him over the cliff at Nazareth because he stood for the truth. I can assure you that we will receive similar treatment if we refuse to sell Jesus' salvation short. But that is the price of truth. Jesus is the truth! He is the long-awaited Messiah who came to set us free from sin. Is it not true love when we are prepared to suffer persecution and even death for blowing the whistle on Christian sinning?

> If ye then be risen with Christ, seek those things which are above, where Christ sitteth on the right hand of God. Set your affection on things above, not on things on the earth. [Reach for the stars.] For ye are dead, and your life is hid with Christ in God. [It is no longer you who lives but Christ.] When Christ, who is our life, shall appear, then shall ye also appear with him in glory. Mortify therefore [put to death, by the Holy Spirit] your members which are upon the earth; fornication [sex outside of a marriage license], uncleanness [sinning], inordinate affection, evil concupiscence [lawlessness], and covetousness, which is idolatry: For which things' sake the wrath of God cometh on the children of disobedience [*the children who are disobedient*]: In the which ye also walked some time, when ye lived in them. But now ye also put off all these [foul deeds]; anger, wrath, malice, blasphemy, filthy communication out of your mouth. Lie not one to another, seeing that ye have put off the old man with his deeds; *And have put on the new man, who is renewed in knowledge*

after the image of Him that created him.

—Colossians 3:1–10

Does this exhortation from the apostle Paul sound like we should give up and accept that we will be sinners until we die? Does it sound like we can expect saints to be sinners at the same time? Are we all doomed to one day commit sin? No! He is emphatic that we are winners and cannot lose. "Reach for the stars," it tells me, and grasp hold of your eternal life. Try it, you'll like it!

Seventy-four chapters from Acts to Revelation warn Christians not to commit sin. On the other hand, only one verse—1 John 2:1—says, "…if any man sin." Why is this verse an all-time favorite with the church? We also nearly always change it to read *when we sin*, and thereby make the poison of sinning a foregone conclusion.

Would you tell your child that a bottle contains deadly poison and say, "When you drink it, call a doctor"? I don't think so. You would be a foolish parent to speak that way. Rather, you would say, "This bottle of poison is not to be touched. However, son, if by some tragic mistake you happen to swallow some, rush to a doctor. He may be able to save your life."

We came to the Lord because we were spiritually dead from drinking the poison called sin. Now, however, we are confronted with an established church that teaches that we will have to continue drinking poison. We leaders do not know of any other way. Yet, we think that we have worked out a way whereby it will not kill us. It might sound as if we are following in Satan's footsteps and giving the same line he gave to Eve when he told her that she would not die if she disobeyed God; however, we have scriptures that we believe support our theory that saints can also be sinners.

Church, how can we do this?

I suggest the following scriptures to remove confusion from the question if saints are also sinners:

And you hath he quickened, who were dead in trespasses and sins: Wherein in time past ye walked according to the course of this world, according to the prince of the power of the air, the spirit that now worketh in the children of disobedience: Among whom also we all had our conversation *in times past* in the lusts of our flesh, fulfilling the desires of the flesh and of the mind; and were by nature the children of wrath, even as others. But God, who is rich in mercy, for his great love wherewith he loved us, Even when we were dead [from the poison of sin], hath quickened us together with Christ...

—EPHESIANS 2:1–5

[He did this by] the exceeding greatness of his power to us-ward who believe, according to the working of his mighty power, Which he wrought in Christ, when he raised him from the dead, and set him at his own right hand in the heavenly places, Far above all principality, and power, and might, and dominion, and every name that is named, not only in this world, but also in that which is to come: And hath put all things under his feet, and gave him to be the head over all things to the church, Which is his body...

—EPHESIANS 1:19–23

That in the ages to come he might show the exceeding riches of his grace in his kindness toward us through Christ Jesus... For through him we... have access by one Spirit unto the Father.

—EPHESIANS 2:7, 18

That ye put off concerning the former conversation the old man, which is corrupt according to the deceitful lusts; And be renewed in the spirit of your mind; And that ye put on [by faith in God's promise] *the new man, who after God is created in righteousness and true holiness.*

—EPHESIANS 4:22–24

But fornication [sex outside of marriage], and all uncleanness, or covetousness, let it not be once named among you, as becometh saints; Neither filthiness, nor foolish talking, nor jesting, which are not convenient: but rather giving of thanks. For this ye know, that no whoremonger [anyone who sells their own body for illegal sex], nor [sinfully] unclean person, nor covetous man [greedy to keep up with 'the Joneses next door], who is an idolater, hath any inheritance in the kingdom of Christ and of God. *Let no man deceive you with vain words: for because of these things cometh the wrath of God upon the children of disobedience.* Be not ye therefore partakers with them. For ye were sometimes darkness, but now are ye light in the Lord: walk as children of light: (For the fruit of the Spirit is in all goodness and righteousness and truth;) Proving what is acceptable unto the Lord. And have no fellowship with the unfruitful works of darkness, *but rather reprove [Christians who are openly sinning]*. For it is a shame even to speak of those things which are done of them in secret.

—EPHESIANS 5:3–12

Wherefore be ye not unwise, but understanding what the will of the Lord is. And be not drunk with wine, wherein is excess; but be filled with the Spirit; Speaking to yourselves in psalms and hymns and spiritual songs, singing and making melody in your heart to the Lord.

—EPHESIANS 5:17–19

[Remember that] Christ is the head of the church: and he is the saviour of [his] body....[and must] present it to himself a glorious church, *not having spot, or wrinkle, or any such thing; but that it should be holy and without blemish.*

—EPHESIANS 5:23, 27

Above all, taking the shield of faith, wherewith ye shall be able to quench all the fiery darts [a temptation to commit sin] of the wicked.

—EPHESIANS 6:16

I do not think any court of law would declare that these scriptures give any impression that believers will be sinners. A brother in the Lord phoned me just last night and told me with great joy that he believes it would be harder for him to sin than to not sin. He is one who has recently accepted by faith the truth of exchanging his own life for Christ's life.

After Jesus returned to heaven, the Holy Spirit fell on thirsty members of His church, according to the promises of John 7:38 and Isaiah 55:1. Many years later, he appeared to John on the island of Patmos and instructed him to write His personal assessment to seven separate churches that had been planted in different locations across what is now the country of Turkey.

You will notice that He never once mentioned nor implied that the church members' future salvation (inheritance) was assured. Instead, he did what He will do when He returns: He assessed their works. Therefore, I believe without a doubt that our eternal salvation depends on our works. To deny this would be an act of denying the validity of the Book of Revelation and the teaching of Jesus in the Gospels. The apostle Paul also taught:

> [God] will render to every man according to his deeds: To them who by patient continuance in well doing seek for glory and honour and immortality, eternal life: But unto them that are contentious, and do not obey the truth, but obey unrighteousness, indignation and wrath, Tribulation and anguish, upon every soul of man that doeth evil, of the Jew first, and also of the Gentile; *But glory, honour, and peace, to every man that worketh good.*
>
> —Romans 2:6–10

Therefore, these early churches would not have been shocked or surprised that Jesus assessed them on their works alone. They would have been wise enough to understand Paul's teachings that their initial deliverance and reconciliation depended not on their works, but on their faith alone. However, their future eternal salvation did depend on the works they did after being reconciled to their heavenly Father.

A study of very early church history shows that it accepted the preceding teaching of Paul. This book is intended to help restore that wisdom to the church before Jesus Christ comes back as our judge. Will you please help me before it is too late?

Let us now study a summary of Christ's message to each of the seven churches in Asia.

To the church at Ephesus:

> I know thy works...Remember therefore from whence thou art fallen, and repent, and do the first works [works of love]; or else I will come unto thee quickly, and will remove thy candlestick [your church] out of his place, except thou repent.
>
> —Revelation 2:2–5

To the church in Smyrna:

> I know *thy work*,...He that hath an ear, let him hear what the Spirit saith unto the churches; He that overcometh [sinful works] shall not be hurt of the second death [the lake of fire].
>
> —Revelation 2:9–11

Read that last sentence again. Just yesterday, a Christian leader called me to say that he was taking a close look at the teaching on the second death. He was finding it very scary.

To the church at Pergamos:

> I know thy works...thou holdest fast my name, and hast not denied my faith...But I have a few things against thee, because thou hast there them that hold [false] doctrine [and lead you into sinful works]...Repent...hear what the Spirit saith unto the churches; To him that overcometh [sinful works] will I give to eat of the hidden manna.
>
> —Revelation 2:13–17

To the church in Thyatira:

> I know thy works, and charity, and service, and faith, and thy patience, and thy works; and the last to be more than the first. Notwithstanding I have a few things against thee, because thou [hast been seduced into sinful works of] fornication, and [eating] things sacrificed unto idols... and I will give unto every one of you according to your works... And he that overcometh, and keepeth my works unto the end, to him will I give power over the nations.
>
> —REVELATION 2:19–26

To the church in Sardis:

> I know thy works, that thou hast a name that thou livest, and art dead. Be watchful, and strengthen the things which remain, that are ready to die: for I have not found thy works perfect before God... Thou hast a few names even in Sardis which have not defiled their garments; and they shall walk with me in white: for they are worthy. He that overcometh, the same shall be clothed in white raiment; and I will not blot out his name out of the book of life... [where it was written at the foundation of the earth, according to Revelation 17:8].
>
> —REVELATION 3:1–5

To the church at Philadelphia:

> I know thy works:... Because thou hast [persevered in doing my word], I also will keep thee from the hour of [trial], which shall come upon all the world,... Him that overcometh [temptations to think or commit sinful works] will I make a pillar in the temple of my God, Only the one who overcomes (temptations to think or commit sinful works) I will make a pillar in the temple of my God.
>
> —REVELATION 3:8–12

To the church of the Laodiceans:

> I know thy works, that thou art neither cold nor hot:...because thou art lukewarm, and neither cold nor hot, I will spue thee out of my mouth. To him that overcometh will I grant to sit with me in my throne, even as I also overcame, and am set down with my Father in his throne. He that hath an ear, let him hear what the Spirit saith unto the churches.
>
> —Revelation 3:15–22

You may read all of the above letters to the seven churches in full in Revelation, chapters 2 and 3. In the light of the whole of the Bible, I believe it would be very rash to assume that eternal salvation (eternal life) does not depend on a Christian's works (deeds). For those of you who think that a Christian's judgment is only concerned with rank in heaven and not eternal salvation, I would point you again to Romans 2:6–11, 1 Peter 1:17, Revelation 2:11 (the church in Smyrna), and Revelation 3:4–5 (the church in Sardis).

Satan easily convinced Eve that sin would not kill her. Are we in a more privileged condition than Eve or Adam before their fall? I believe not! Where is one's rank after having been spewed out of the Master's mouth?

Matthew 19:16–22 tells about a young man who had many possessions and asked Jesus how he could gain eternal life (eternal salvation). Jesus did not ask the man about his faith, but immediately questioned him about sinful works. Jesus accepted the reply that as far as the young man knew he had not transgressed the Law. But the man was still not satisfied and asked, "What more do I lack?"

This gave Jesus the opportunity to teach that if we want more than our inheritance of eternal life, there is a degree of perfection that can only be reached by discarding all worldly attachments. He said: "If thou wilt be perfect, go and sell that thou hast, and give to the poor, and thou shalt have treasure in heaven: and come and follow me." The rich man declined Christ's offer to be perfect, but he did not decline salvation.

The Jews well knew that their eternal salvation depended on their deeds being righteous, so they tried to be righteous by the Law. At His death, Jesus gave us a *New* Testament that says eternal salvation is still dependent on a person's righteous works (Rev. 19:8; Rom. 2:6–11). To enable us to obtain this righteous lifestyle, the new and successful unwritten law of the Spirit of life in Christ Jesus has replaced the old and unsuccessful Law of Moses. For if righteousness could come by the Law only, then Christ died in vain.

> For what the law could not do, in that it was weak through the flesh, God sending his own Son in the likeness of sinful flesh, and for sin, condemned sin in the flesh: That the righteousness of the law might be fulfilled in us, who walk not after the flesh, but after the Spirit.
>
> —ROMANS 8:3–4

It is, of course, impossible to please God without faith, whether we are under the Law of Moses in the Old Testament or the New Testament. I am writing to show that the working-out and acceptance of the New Testament is entirely dependent on God's grace and our choice to not frustrate its operation. God's grace is Him operating in our lives, His way, by the Spirit of grace. Woe to us if we frustrate that grace by trying to do it our way!

> Until the Spirit be poured upon us from on high, and the wilderness be a fruitful field...and righteousness remain in the fruitful field. And the work of righteousness shall be peace; and the effect of righteousness quietness and assurance for ever.
>
> —ISAIAH 32:16–17

Chapter 7

For Little Children, Everything Is Pure

I read recently of a Christian who said he would not go into a motel room until the television set has been removed and also of another who can no longer go to the beach because of the girls. They called it obeying God. But Jesus taught that unless we become as little children, we cannot be admitted to His eternal kingdom. Little children are not ensnared by immorality on television nor adversely affected by the girls at the beach. Jesus came to set us free from being slaves to sin. If we are walking in His Spirit, we have His mind, which is childlike.

The Jews taught the people to avoid the occasions of sin. Jesus shocked them by eating and drinking in places where there were prostitutes, extortioners, sinners, and heavy drinkers. He was walking in the Spirit of His Father. He did not make firm friends with sinners, but He was friendly toward them so that He could save some. He was a walking overcomer, who had the victory over all temptations. He was born free from the power of sin in His flesh, and He came to give us the same type of life. He took us to death, freed us from sin, and filled us with His Spirit.

In Christ, we are able to overcome all temptations and to be like little children amidst the temptations of the world. Temptations are defanged for us as we walk by faith in His Spirit. We are new creations. Beware of those who teach that we need to avoid the occasions of sin, for they have not experienced His freedom. They would put you back into bondage. Paul spoke of this childlike freedom, which He possessed in his walk in the Spirit when he declared, "All things are lawful unto me, but all things are not expedient" (1 Cor. 6:12). This was the way Jesus walked.

Test yourself. Evaluate if you are walking by faith in the Spirit of Christ Jesus by going to the beach and seeing if you are like the little children. If you are not, it is time to fear and return to your first love until once again, your works and thoughts are pure. Anyone born of God cannot sin. I am not boasting, because without Him I can do nothing. I have a television set in my home, and I have not watched it for the past thirty years. I have had no inclination to do so since the day Christ baptized me with the Holy Spirit and with the fire of His love. It is so much better than wine—or television!

Anyone who abides in Christ does not commit sin, because in Him we are overcomers of temptations to sin. We are not sons of God with a future inheritance of eternal life unless we are being led of the Spirit of God daily. If we cannot go to certain places for fear of sinning, we are in bondage, and Paul reminds us in Galatians 4:30 that the son of the bondwoman is cast out. Jesus showed us to overcome evil with good. Walk in the Spirit and we will not obey the desires of the flesh. When we walk in the Spirit, we walk as innocent little children. Jesus spoke harsh words against any who scandalize these little children and said, "It is better for him that a millstone were hanged about his neck, and he were cast into the sea" (Mark 9:42). Teachers beware!

Paul, Peter, and John each have a continuing theme—that of a future salvation and our need to be careful that we do not miss it—in all of their letters to the church. To this end, they warn us against living a sinful and doubting lifestyle.

In Titus 2:11–13, Paul writes:

> For the grace of God that bringeth salvation hath appeared to all men, Teaching us that, denying ungodliness and worldly lusts, we should live soberly, righteously [sinlessly], and Godly, in this present world; Looking for that blessed hope [of future salvation], and the glorious appearing of the great God and our Saviour Jesus Christ.

Jesus gave Himself for us to redeem us from all evil and purify unto Himself a special people who are eager to do good works.

> This is a faithful saying, and these things I will that thou affirm constantly, that they which have believed in God might be careful to maintain good works.
>
> —Titus 3:8

> For we are his workmanship, created in Christ Jesus unto good works, which God hath before ordained that we should walk in them.
>
> —Ephesians 2:10

Romans 2:6 and 1 Peter 1:17 offer further teaching on this. Be careful of your lifestyle, Christian. As Titus 1:16 says, some "profess that they know God; but in works they deny him."

Second Timothy 4:1 teaches that the Lord Jesus Christ will judge both the living and the dead when He comes again with His kingdom. Therefore, in 2 Timothy 2:10, Paul says that he endures "all things" for those called to be Christ's, so that they may "obtain the salvation which is in Christ Jesus with eternal glory." He adds:

> Reprove, rebuke, exhort with all longsuffering and doctrine. For the time will come when they will not endure sound doctrine; but after their own lusts [sinful desires] shall they heap to themselves teachers, having itching ears; And they shall turn away [their] ears from the truth, and shall be turned unto fables [false worldly wisdom and legendary tales].
>
> —2 TIMOTHY 4:2–4

> In meekness instructing those that oppose themselves; if God peradventure will give them repentance to the acknowledging of the truth; And that they may recover themselves out of the snare of the devil, who are taken captive by him at his will.
>
> —2 TIMOTHY 2:25–26

Paul is comparing Christians to the nation of Israel when he writes:

> Because of unbelief they were broken off, and thou standest by faith. Be not highminded, but fear [be mindful of the danger]: For if God spared not the natural branches [the Jews], take heed lest he also spare not thee. Behold therefore the goodness and severity of God: on them which fell, severity; but toward thee, goodness, *if thou continue in his goodness: otherwise thou also shalt be cut off.*
>
> —ROMANS 11:20–22

According to Hebrews 6:4–6, we should know that it is impossible for Christians "who were once enlightened, and have tasted of the heavenly gift [of the Holy Spirit]... and the good word of God and [supernatural] powers [of the gifts of the Spirit], if they shall fall away, to renew them again unto repentance; *seeing they crucify to themselves the Son of God afresh, and put him to an open shame.*"

It is impossible for them to be reconciled again because they sin against the Holy Spirit of grace. They are in the race but have become disqualified and cannot win their inheritance of eternal life (Heb. 12:14). Second Timothy 2:5 teaches that a man can strive to win, but he is "not crowned, except he strive lawfully [without sinning]."

Colossians 1:21 says that we were God's enemies before conversion because of our sinful works:

> Yet now hath he reconciled [us] In the body of his flesh through death, to present [us] holy and unblameable and unreproveable in his sight: If [we] continue in the faith.
>
> —Colossians 1:21–23

We win if we walk by faith in the promise that the law of the Spirit of life in Christ Jesus has set us free from the law of having to sin, with its punishment of eternal death. We know too that without a holy lifestyle, we will not see God. Our lifestyle reveals the reality or the pretence of our faith, and therefore God judges us on our works. Matthew 12:33 explains that "the tree is known by his fruit."

As we read Genesis 2:7, we can conclude that Adam and his wife Eve were both Spirit-filled. Also, they were both under God's grace, according to Genesis 1:28. In Genesis 2:9, we see that they both had access to the tree of life—the promise of eternal life. And Genesis 3:2–3 and 17 show that they both knew that God expected them to be obedient, and if not they would die.

All Spirit-filled Christians have the same kind of relationship with God. We have His Spirit, we are under His grace, we have the promise of eternal life in Christ, and we *should* know that the wages of disobedience is death.

It is understandable that the two in the Garden of Eden might easily think God's grace would cover their disobedient act of eating the fruit of the knowledge of good and evil. God obviously loved them. Also, the friendly serpent had assured Eve that she would not die from eating the appealing fruit and had said it would open their eyes to know good and evil. Now how could God be against that? Yes, God did love them, but He had to stand on His word to them. He justly punished their disobedient act with banishment and death.

Dear Christian, you too may have been tricked into believing that because God loves you and you are under His grace, your act of disobedience—which you inwardly know to be sinful—will not result in banishment and spiritual death. But God has not changed. His Word was, is, and always will be a warning that deliberate sinning is punished by spiritual death. Christ's blood sacrifice atoned for all of our past sins and reconciled us to God. In Christ, we became second Adams and Eves (1 Cor. 15:45–47).

Please be careful not to follow the bad example of Adam and Eve. Do not believe the lie that grace and love will cover our disobedient, willful sinning, but heed the warning of Hebrews 10:26. If, in all honesty, you do not know that your sin is in disobedience to God, you can trust that Jesus will intercede for you according to 1 John 2:1. You can be forgiven, for your sin was not willful. But be careful. As Jeremiah 17:9 says, our own hearts are "desperately wicked" and cunning like the serpent's in the Garden of Eden.

The apostle Peter warns us about how easily we can be tricked. He writes:

> But [in the Old Testament days] there were false prophets also among the people, even as there shall be false teachers among you, who privily shall bring in damnable

heresies, even denying the Lord that bought them, and bring upon themselves swift destruction. And many shall follow their pernicious [fatal] ways; by reason of whom the way of truth [Christianity] shall be evil spoken of. And through covetousness shall they with feigned [forged] words make merchandise of you [trick you]... [But] if *God spared not the angels that sinned*, but cast them down to hell, and delivered them into chains of darkness, to be reserved unto judgment; And spared not the old world, but saved Noah the eighth [person], a preacher of righteousness, bringing in the flood upon the world of the ungodly; And turning the cities of Sodom and Gomorrha into ashes condemned them with an overthrow, making them an example unto those that after should live [un-Godly] [sinfully]; And delivered just Lot, vexed [distraught] with the filthy conversation of the wicked... The Lord knoweth how to deliver the godly out of temptations, and to reserve the unjust unto the day of judgment to be punished.

—2 Peter 2:1–9

And [these false teachers] shall receive the reward of unrighteousness... Spots they are and blemishes, sporting themselves with their own deceivings [that God's grace covers their sinning] while they feast with you; Having eyes full of adultery, and that cannot cease from sin.

—2 Peter 2:13–14

These are wells without water, clouds that are carried with a tempest; to whom the mist of darkness is reserved for ever... For if after they have escaped the pollutions of the world through the knowledge of the Lord and Saviour Jesus Christ, they are again entangled therein, and overcome, the latter end is worse [than before their deliverance in Christ]. *For it had been better for them not to have known the way of righteousness, than, after they have*

> *known it, to turn from the holy commandment delivered unto them.* But it is happened unto them according to the true proverb, The dog is turned to his own vomit again.
>
> —2 PETER 2:17, 20–22

Therefore beloved, beware lest you also are led away by erroneous teaching and fall from your own steadfastness. They promise you liberty but they themselves are bond slaves to sin.

But there were false prophets also among the people, even as there shall be false teachers among you, who privily shall bring in damnable heresies, even denying the Lord that bought them, and bring upon themselves swift destruction (2 Pet. 2:1). They are throughout the present-day church denying that Jesus has set us free from sin and sinning.

God requires that His Son's bride be spotless and without blemish in lifestyle. Jesus told a parable about a wedding dinner a king had prepared for his Son and said that a man came in without a wedding garment. He taught that the King of glory will say to His servants, "Bind that man hand and foot, and take him away, and cast him into outer darkness; there shall be weeping and gnashing of teeth [in anger and frustration of having been deceived]" (Matt. 22:13).

It sounds easy and assuring when Jesus says in John 5:24: "He that heareth my word, and believeth on him that sent me, hath everlasting life, and shall not come into condemnation; but is passed from death unto life." However, the phrase *to hear* means not just to know Christ's promises, but also to do them. For He Himself said:

> Not every one that saith unto me, Lord, Lord, shall enter into the kingdom of heaven; but he that doeth the will of my Father which is in heaven... And every one that heareth these sayings of mine, and doeth them not, shall be likened unto a foolish man, which built his house upon the sand: And the rain descended, and the floods came, and the winds blew, and beat upon

> that house; and it fell: and great was the fall of it.
>
> —Matthew 7:21, 26–27

> Beware of false prophets, which come to you in sheep's clothing, but inwardly they are ravening wolves... A good tree cannot bring forth evil fruit, neither can a corrupt tree bring forth good fruit... Wherefore by their fruits ye shall know them.
>
> —Matthew 7:15, 18, 20

The apostle Paul says, "We are [God's] workmanship, created in Christ Jesus unto good works, which God hath before ordained that we should walk in them" (Eph. 2:10). Jesus identifies these good works in Matthew 25:31–46, when He tells how He will return to separate the sheep from the goats on Judgment Day. They consist of feeding the hungry and thirsty, caring for wayfarers, clothing the poor, and visiting the sick and the prisoners. We will be judged on these works as worthy or unworthy to enter into the inheritance of the kingdom prepared before the earth was created (1 Pet. 1:17).

> Marvel not at this: for the hour is coming, in the which all that are in the graves [*all* includes Christians] shall hear his voice, And shall come forth; *they that have done good, unto the resurrection of life; and they that have done evil, unto the resurrection of damnation* [in the lake of eternal fire, according to Revelation 20:12–15]... these things I say, that ye might be saved.
>
> —John 5:28–29, 34

Many churches commonly accept the belief that Christians will not have to face judgment. Jesus said that an obedient, Spirit-filled believer "does not come into judgment" (John 5:24, RSV). However, it must be understood that the word *judgment* means "the sentence of a court of justice." It cannot mean that we will not be judged because Paul taught in 2 Corinthians 5:10 that we must all appear before the judgment seat of Christ. The King James Version clarifies John 5:24 by using the word *condemnation* rather than the word *judgment*. This, of course, agrees with Paul's teaching in Romans 8:1-2 that there is no condemnation to those who have been freed from sin and its punishment—death—by the law of the Spirit of life in Christ Jesus.

To draw the conclusion from Scripture that Christians will not have to face their judge is simply another trick that Satan has inspired to lure souls to hell. Hopefully the Christian's works will allow them to hear the words of their judge—Jesus—saying "Well done, thou good and faithful servant" (Matt. 25:21).

It may not be fashionable to mention hell from the pulpit, but Jesus repeatedly warned God's people about it. He taught:

> And if thy hand [leads you to sin], cut it off [He meant it]: it is better for thee to enter into life maimed, than having two hands to go into hell, into the fire that never shall be quenched: Where [the spiritual] worm dieth not, and the [spiritual] fire is not quenched. And if thy foot [leads you to commit sin], cut it off: it is better for thee to [be a cripple in order to win eternal life], than having two feet to be cast into hell...Where their worm dieth not, and the fire is not quenched. And if thine eye [leads you to sin], pluck it out: it is better for thee to enter into the kingdom of God with one eye, than having two eyes to be cast into hell fire: Where their worm dieth not, and the fire is not quenched.
>
> —MARK 9:43–48

Jesus sees into hell and understands the endless horror and pain of being eaten by worms and burned by fire. If the beach causes you to sin, do not think that you will win over sin by avoiding it, but pluck out your eye. However, if you are walking in the Spirit of Christ according to Romans 8:4, your heart will be right and your eye will not be evil, no matter what you see. In other words, do not throw out your TV set!

Down through the church age, different saints have had visions of hell, and some have experienced the trauma and pain of it. It is the place of punishment God created for the rebellious angels. We must also be aware that it is the place of punishment for sinners who die in their sins. Only those who live righteously avoid hell! This book is written to show us how to live righteously and avoid hell.

Paul, Peter, and John never stopped warning us how to avoid being like the pig that is lured back so easily to the mud pile.

> Perverse disputings of men of corrupt minds, and destitute of the truth, supposing that gain [of money or possessions] is godliness: *from such withdraw thyself*… And having food and raiment let us be therewith content. [In the West today, the big problem seems to be: unable to wear clothing, because of consuming too much food.] But they that will be rich fall into temptation and a snare, and into many foolish and hurtful lusts, which drown men in destruction and perdition. For the love of money is the root of all evil: which while some coveted after, they have erred from the faith, and pierced themselves through with many sorrows. But thou, O man of God, flee these things; and follow after righteousness, godliness, faith, love, patience, meekness…lay hold on [grasp] eternal life,…keep [the will of God] without spot, unrebukeable [blameless],…until the appearing of our Lord Jesus Christ:…Charge them that are rich in this world, that they be not highminded, nor trust in uncertain riches, but in the living God,…That they do good, that they be rich in good works, ready to distribute [generous], willing to communicate [share with the needy]; *Laying up in store for themselves a good foundation [of good works] against the time to come, that they may lay hold on eternal life*…avoiding profane and vain babblings [about how to be wealthy, trim, taut, and terrific], and oppositions of science falsely so called [such as man should stop filling (replenishing) the earth with people].
>
> —1 Timothy 6:5–21

These warnings from Paul concern where we will spend eternity. He and I want to see you in heaven.

In 1 Thessalonians 5:23, Paul prayed that the Thessalonians might continuously live a blameless lifestyle—spirit, soul, and body. How does this sit with the false teaching that our future salvation is unconditionally assured? His prayer in Philippians 1.10 was "that ye may be sincere and without offence till the day of Christ."

Paul told us why he prayed for the churches:

> Put on the whole armour of God, that ye may be able to stand against the wiles of the devil. For we wrestle not against flesh and blood, but against principalities, against powers, against the rulers of the darkness of this world,… Wherefore take unto you the whole armour of God, that ye may be able to withstand in the evil day, and having done all, to stand… Praying always with all prayer and supplication in the Spirit, and watching thereunto with all perseverance and supplication for all saints.
>
> —Ephesians 6:11–13, 18

Galatians 3:11 teaches that we must have a lifestyle of faith to be just before God. Romans 1:16–18 says that salvation and righteousness is "revealed from faith to faith" and God's wrath is revealed from heaven against all ungodliness and unrighteousness of men, who hold the truth in unrighteousness.

In 1 John 1:6 and 2:4, the apostle John says that we Christians are liars if we think we know God and have fellowship with Him but do not obey Him. First Peter 3:13–14 reminds us that we are looking forward to new heavens and a new earth, where all is righteousness. Therefore, Peter tells us to be diligent that He will find us in peace, without spot and blameless. It is true that all who call on the name of the Lord will be reconciled to God. However, from then on, our eternal salvation demands that we be holy, without spot, and blameless. In Matthew 7:22–23, Jesus said that many will cry, "Lord, Lord," but He will say, "I never knew you."

Eternal salvation is not cheap. Let us be most careful that we are not led away with the error of the wicked and fall from steadfastness to Christ in our lifestyle. Remember that Eve, in Genesis 3:4, was led away by the deception that she would not die if she disobeyed God. But God says in Romans 6:23 that "the wages of sin *is* death." Eve disobeyed God and instantly suffered spiritual death.

It is true that we do not become reconciled to God on the basis of our works, for all have sinned, according to Romans 3:23. However, it is undeniable that our eternal salvation is determined on our works. In 1 Corinthians 6:9, we see that although the church at Corinth were Spirit-filled Christians, many soon forgot that unrighteous Christians will not inherit the kingdom of God. Sound familiar?

Perhaps it is very easy for us to feel sorry for ourselves when any adversity comes our way. We may bemoan our condition and even burst into tears. But on the other hand, we cannot shed a tear for those who are going to hell by their unbelief and sinning. We may offer a prayer or two, but where is the deep sorrow and tears that our Savior expressed for them? Have we been numbed into thinking that maybe their sins are not all that bad, and maybe hell is not a real place? Do we have the heart of Christ if we do not offer our bodies and their woes as "a living sacrifice, holy, acceptable unto God"? (Rom. 12:1).

Please join me in this prayer:

> *Take my heart, O Lord. Fill it with one accord with Yours. Take it, shake it, break it, remake it, until it is one with Yours. Take over, Holy Spirit. Pour more of Your wine of love and compassion into my heart. Amen.*

We are now on our way to having a heart of flesh, which cares more for others than self in the spiritual realm. We may suffer terrible agonies when our wife or children are stricken with sickness or pain, but we seem able to be quite calm, patient, and in control when our children or brothers and sisters are living in sin or unbelief. Have we lost our sense of reality? The pains of hell are infinitely worse than any physical pain— even worse than having an eye gouged out—and they continue for all eternity. Reality is concerned with eternity rather than day-to-day happenings. Death can come suddenly at any age, and it plunges us, ready or not, into eternity. It is a tragedy for anyone to die in their sins. Where is our love if we fail to warn them and cry out to God for them night and day? It is our responsibility, not His!

It is wrong to imagine that our tears will rob us of our joy. Both sorrow and joy come from the same love that is poured from God's heart into ours, and God has a time and a season for both of them, according to Ecclesiastes 3.4. Wait on Him. Do not work up your own sorrow or joy. He will kiss us in His time, as described in Song of Solomon 1:2 and 3:5, and we will cry in His time. It is the Christian lifestyle of God's sons; in which we are led by the Spirit of Jesus Christ our Lord. Worldly sorrow leads to depression and death, but Godly sorrow leads to repentance and life, as 2 Corinthians 7:10 says.

Reading the Old Testament is a good way to remind us to not drift off into a stupor whereby we forget God's *severity,* even though it may be delayed in coming. First Corinthians 10:1–12 offers us a specific lesson concerning the nation of Israel. Let us not be ignorant of the way God's people were led out of captivity from Egypt under a cloud. All passed through the sea; and all were baptized into Moses in the cloud and in the sea. They all ate the same spiritual food and drank the same spiritual drink of the Rock, which was Christ. But with most of them, God was not pleased, and He destroyed them in the wilderness.

Now these things are an example for us Christians. Let us not be idolaters, who spend all their free time in working, partying, and playing sports. Neither let us commit sins such as sexual relations outside of marriage. When the people of Israel tried it in the wilderness, God killed twenty-three thousand of them in one day. Let us not put God to the test by presuming on His goodness. When they did this, God sent snakes to bite them, and many died. And we must not grumble and complain to God, for the destroyer destroyed those who did so. All these things are in the Bible for our admonition and warning.

Therefore, let the Christian who thinks that he stands immovable take heed lest he fall. No Christian is above falling to destruction. The physical punishment of death in the Old Testament is a picture of spiritual death for New Testament believers. Does the teaching of 1 Corinthians 10:1–12 remotely suggest that our eternal salvation (inheritance) is assured? It is apparent that as God's people wandered in the desert, they were foolish enough, like their first parents, to presume on God's goodness and forget that the promise of the land of milk and honey was not unconditional. To think that it was brought disaster.

The church of today is already seeing the horrors that we have brought upon ourselves and the next generation by the deception which has led us to believe that our future is assured in His goodness, regardless of our works. How can we do this, church? It is not too late to blow the whistle and call a halt. By His grace, we still have time to start again.

Let us return to a lifestyle of working out our salvation with fear and trembling because it is almighty God Himself who is working in us so that we will be doers of His will. And let us be very careful to do everything without complaining so that we may be blameless and harmless in this crooked world system, which is inside and outside the church. By so doing, we may rejoice that our race was not run in vain on that day when we are judged by Christ, for we will have run with patience the race that was set before us.

Hebrews 12:3 reminds us to "consider him [Jesus our Lord] that endured such contradiction of sinners against himself, lest ye be wearied and faint in your minds." I have received endless opposition to the writing of this and my previous book, *Go And*

Sin No More. Many times I have been tempted to succumb to my opponents and faint at the task which God has given me.

However, Hebrews 12:6–11 offers us the following encouragement:

> For whom the Lord loveth he chasteneth, and scourgeth every son whom he receiveth. If ye endure chastening, God dealeth with you as with sons; for what son is he whom the father chasteneth not? But if ye be without chastisement, whereof all are partakers, then are ye bastards [illegitimate], and not sons. Furthermore we have had fathers of our flesh which corrected us, and we gave them reverence: shall we not much rather be in subjection unto the Father of spirits, and live? For they verily for a few days chastened us after their own pleasure; but He for our profit, that we might be partakers of His holiness. Now no chastening for the present seemeth to be joyous, but grievous: nevertheless afterward it yieldeth the peaceable fruit of righteousness [holiness].

Chastisement tests our obedience and our patience. James 1:3–4 teaches that this "trying of your faith worketh patience. But let patience have her perfect work, that ye may be perfect and entire, wanting nothing."

> I the Lord have called thee in righteousness, and will hold thine hand, and will keep thee, and give thee for a covenant of the people...To open the blind eyes, to bring out the prisoners from the prison, and them that sit in darkness out of the prison house.
>
> —Isaiah 42:6–7

Chapter 8

A Reformation of Righteousness Through Love

COLOSSIANS 1:13 TEACHES that God "hath delivered us from the power of darkness and hath translated us into the kingdom of his dear Son," so that we, by obeying His rule, may obtain eternal salvation on Judgment Day. The fruit produced in obeying the Spirit of Jesus Christ is "holiness and [its] end everlasting life" (Rom. 6:21–22). When we are in the kingdom of darkness, we obey its ruler, Satan; and our end is the lake of fire forever.

If the church would understand and accept the paragraph you just read, it would experience a reformation and become the spotless bride of Christ on earth. The church would be a bride prepared to meet her King-Husband in the clouds. I suggest that you read the previous paragraph again—slowly, chewing and digesting it.

Restoring Righteousness

The worldwide outpouring of the Holy Spirit in the last century came as Elijah to prepare us to enter this coming reformation—a reformation of truth and righteousness that will be marked by the unity of the Spirit, not splintering division. The only division will be our separation from the world, the flesh, and the devil. It will be the coming apart from Babylon.

In Matthew 13:36–43, Jesus explained the meaning of the parable of the weeds of the field. His words teach us that the day is coming when He will send His angels into His kingdom:

> …and they shall gather out of his kingdom all things that offend [those who teach others that it is all right to sin], and them which do iniquity [those who are sinning]; And shall cast them into a furnace of fire: there shall be wailing and gnashing of teeth. *Then shall the righteous shine forth as the sun in the kingdom of their Father.*

Dear Reader, are you teaching a grace that winks at sinning? Are you sinning? Are you so foolish as to believe that the saints can also be sinners? This may be your last chance to turn from being chaff to wheat. When His angels come, it will be too late to change.

Jesus, speaking to a people under the old covenant of the Law, identified four things that are required for entry into the eternal kingdom of heaven:

1. "Except a man be born of water and of the Spirit, he cannot enter into the kingdom of God" (John 3:5).

2. "For God so loved the world, that he gave his only begotten Son, that whosoever believeth in him should…have everlasting life" (John 3:16).

3. "…if thou wilt enter into life, keep the commandments" (Matt. 19:17).

4. Come, ye blessed of my Father, inherit the kingdom prepared for you from the foundation of the world: For I was an hungered, and ye gave me meat: I was thirsty, and ye gave me drink: I was a stranger, and ye took me in: Naked, and ye clothed me: I was sick, and ye visited me: I was in prison, and ye came unto me... Inasmuch as ye have done it unto one of the least of these my brethren, ye have done it unto me" (Matthew 25:34–40).

This book has drawn from the New Testament writers—Luke (in the Book of Acts), and Paul, Peter, John, and Jude (in their letters). It explains how these four things are fulfilled by believers who are baptized into Christ by water and baptized by Christ with the Holy Spirit (Acts 10:44–48). These believers walk, believing and confessing that it is not we who live, but Christ (Rom. 10:9-10, Gal. 2:19–20). They walk in holiness, obeying the leading of His Spirit (Rom. 8:14, Heb. 12:14).

It would be very strange to imagine that a walking-in-the-Spirit Christian could commit sin. Hereby know we that we live in God and He in us because He has given us the Person who is His Spirit. There is a big difference between believing I have the Holy Spirit and knowing it. I can only know it by an experience.

According to the Book of Acts and the testimony of people who have been caught up in the last fifty years of Charismatic-Pentecostal "personal downloadings of Holy Spirit love power," the Spirit comes in with an unforgettable experience of God's love. Only the Holy Spirit can give God's love to us. The Holy Spirit is the Spirit of God. God is love; and the one who loves cannot sin. The apostle John says the reason we cannot sin is that God's seed is in us. That seed is God's love. We know that we have passed from death to life because we love the brethren. First John 4:7 teaches that everyone who loves is born of God. He who lives in love lives in God, and God in him. Little wonder that the Book of Proverbs claims that love covers a multitude of sins. Paul says that loving our neighbor fulfils all of God's laws.

I was a believer from the age of six, but I did not receive the Holy Spirit until I was forty-eight. He came into me in wave after wave of warm spasms of love. That love transformed me, and I lost all desire for the pleasures of sin that had dogged me all my life.

For many years now, I have found that my life in the Spirit alternates between walking by faith and experiencing His love. When He withdraws His kisses, I have to believe and confess that it is no longer I who live, but Christ by His Spirit in me. But even when I am walking by faith alone, I can constantly feel His love gently simmering deep inside me like a kettle on a stove.

When He kisses me, I can say nothing but "O my Jesus, my Jesus." It lasts for an hour or two and comes in His times, never mine. It is always by His grace. I make sure that I do not frustrate His love. I do not get interested in things of the world. If I seek nothing but His love, I never lose contact with Him. I know that I know that without His love, I will not be able to live righteously. Sometimes He allows the devil to cruelly afflict me with agonies of pain and test my faith. I try then to joyfully offer my body as a living sacrifice. I sympathize with Job and the cry of his heart in Job chapters 28–31.

When the time comes for me to die, I want to be sure that I am living a righteous and sinless lifestyle. Therefore I never risk dying in my sins. I am determined to live so that I will be allowed into His eternal kingdom. First John 4:16–18 explains that we have no fear of going to hell when we are in His love because we cannot but obey our beloved Lord. For this reason, His perfect love casts out all fear of punishment. We know that God cannot condemn us because, when we walk in the Spirit, we walk in "love-works," which are sinless; love-works are good works. But we always retain the holy and awesome fear of our majestic God, who rules the universe through His Son.

If a man resists God's love for his brother, he falls into sinning.

Romans 6:23 says that "the wages of sin [is] death." The love of God is operating in my life when I find myself obeying Jesus Christ and doing His will revealed in the Commandments. Personally, I find that it is not hard to do this because I love to love my Lover. I cannot disobey Him unless I turn my back on His love and go after other lovers who offer worldly pleasures. I would be very foolish to seek anyone or anything apart from Him. His love is so much better than wine.

God commands us to love our brothers. He pours the Holy Spirit into our hearts so that we may do love-works to our brothers and thereby be awarded our inheritance of eternal life. Hebrews 11:6 teaches, "But without faith it is impossible to please [God]." Nothing avails but faith working through love. All the fruit of the Spirit identified in Galatians 5:22–23 simply grows as offshoots of His love.

Paul's faith in God was misdirected until God's love struck him down. Are we not all the same as Paul? I know that I was! I lived on misdirected faith until His Spirit brought me His love.

The two on the road to Emmaus were at the point of losing their faith until God's love began to burn in their hearts. Peter's faith had failed until one look of love pierced his soul and brought lasting repentance. In the twentieth century, every wave of Holy Spirit revival—from Azusa Street to Toronto, Pensacola, Sunderland, and Smithton— birthed new songs of God's love. In the house churches inside China, over six hundred magnificent songs of praise called *Canaan Hymns* were birthed by the Holy Spirit through one peasant girl.

A typical song says. "When we all bow down, Kings will surrender their crowns and worship Jesus, for He is the love, the unfailing love of God." Others cry out, "I love your love" or "I can sing of your love forever." The list of such Spirit-led love songs is endless.

We connect to God's love by faith, but even our faith is a gift from His love. Paul, speaking by the Spirit of Christ, says that love is greater than faith, and faith without love is of no value.

Only those who have not yet been touched and overwhelmed by God's love would find it hard to understand what he is saying. God's grace is God's love gift to us. Every divine healing of the sick is carried out by the power of God's love ministered in Jesus' name, by the Holy Spirit. Nearly all those who are healed tell of the sensation of the warmth of His love as it touches them. Jesus Christ is the seed of God, and that seed is love. Only the works born of love are righteous. Only the Holy Spirit can pour God's love into our hearts. The Father draws us to His Son with cords of love.

If we need more of God's love—and who doesn't—we can ask the Holy Spirit to give it to us. If we need healing in our bodies, we can ask the Holy Spirit to provide it; He brings Christ's love, which is the Father's love. This is the love that caused Jesus to die for us, the love that caused His Father to offer His Son as a sacrifice unto death on a cross. If we need eternal salvation, we simply obey the Spirit of love within us. If we need the Holy Spirit, we can ask Jesus! The Holy Spirit brings God's power, for He brings His love. God's power is His love.

Jesus warned His followers to wait in Jerusalem until the Holy Spirit brought them love-power from on high. When we walk in the Spirit of Jesus Christ, we are walking in God's love. God's love is an experience that produces the good works He requires of us if we are to be eternally saved. Nothing avails but faith working through love.

Just before Jesus returned to heaven, He told His followers in John 15:26 that He would send them another to comfort them as He had done. He said the new comforter would be the Holy Spirit—His Spirit! It is this person, the Spirit of God, who binds together those who have Him in true unity. This unity is the mark of the Spirit. It is not dependent on a formal structure or written regulations; it is a living unity founded and maintained by His love in action.

The following scriptures will help you to understand how the comforter leads us into all truth and eternal salvation: Romans

8:2, 4; 1 John 4:13; Acts 2, 8, 10 and 19; Romans 5:5, 8:9 and 13:10; 1 John 3:9, 14, 4:7, 16–18; Proverbs 10:12; Romans 13:9; Galatians 2:20; 1 Corinthians 13; Revelation 14:7; Romans 6:32; Ezekiel 16:36; Ezekiel 23; Song of Solomon 4:10; Romans 1:17; Galatians 5:6, 22–23; Luke 11:13; Acts 1:4, 8; Ephesians 2:10; 1 Peter 1:17; 2 Peter 1:3, 13; John 14:16, 26, 15:26, 16:7.

The New Testament would not be a better covenant than the old covenant of Moses' Law if it did not set us free from sin and sinning. That is the truth. The New Covenant is the way of righteousness. (Hebrews 5:13; John 8:34, 36; Romans 5:10; *Go and Sin No More*[1].)

Our Savior, Jesus Christ, purchased the New Covenant by His suffering and death. It came into operation at the first Pentecost after He ascended back to His Father in heaven.

I had a personal Pentecostal experience of the Holy Spirit of Jesus coming inside and who continue to walk in the Spirit. It started for me in 1975 on the night I received my personal Pentecost. Pride and worldly dignity disappeared. Pomp and ceremony have no part in a Holy Spirit walk. We pray in unknown tongues of angels or men, and the world says, "You're crazy." That's right! We're crazy about the Lord. If we are crazy about Jesus, it is because we are led by the Spirit. The Father's purpose is that His Spirit witness to us about His glorified Son. We cannot be sure that we possess His Spirit unless we experience His love.

Our future inheritance stands or falls on what we do. Paul tells us to do everything for the Lord wholeheartedly, for we are servants of the Lord Christ. He is the one who will either give us our inheritance of eternal life or else wrong for the wrong we have done. Many Christians have their lives centered around what they eat and drink and are proud of their misdeeds instead of being ashamed. Their minds rotate about earthly things such as clothes, health, sports, news items, gadgets, gossip, Web-surfing (downloading from the Internet rather than the Holy Spirit), family, job, money, cars, houses, and lands. They are continually distracted from heavenly things and the return of the Lord Jesus Christ. Philippians 3:18–19 says that destruction awaits those who show by their deeds that they are enemies of the cross of Christ.

Our deeds are a true reflection of our faith and love. Jesus our judge will have no alternative but to take the axe of destruction and lay it to the roots of the tree that has bad fruit (works). This is why we are judged on our works. Good fruit shows our judge that we walked as He required, by faith working through love.

Many are taught that works do not count in the final washup, but that is the deception of Lucifer. We know that he used it to deceive Eve in the Garden of Eden. In the end, God looks at our works and not on our pleas for forgiveness or mercy. Colossians 3:25 says that "he that doeth wrong shall receive for the wrong which he hath done, and there is no respect of persons." We speak of saints and of sinners, but God does not consider these titles when He makes judgment.

When God says that He will not rub a name out of the Book of Life, He is warning us that He certainly will do it unless we are overcomers. We treat God as a clown, not as a responsible Father, when we claim unconditionally that He won't rub us out of the Book of Life. We are making our own judgments, presuming on His goodness and distorting His warning to the church at Sardis in Revelation 3:5. Jesus is judging the people in the Sardis church on their works. It is not surprising that the Christians of our day lead the field in the popular sins of divorce and remarriage and are not far behind in the abominations of homosexuality and pornography. They have been taught that their names *cannot* be blotted out of the Lamb's Book of Life. What irresponsible and foolish teaching that is!

Again we hear Lucifer's deception that we will not die if we sin. But God's voice thunders, "The wages of sinning is eternal death," and "Hear My beloved Son, in whom I am well pleased." When we Christians do not heed His voice, our children thumb their noses at marriage and live in fornication without shame. Have we gone mad? Even the uncivilized, murderous headhunters, when they were discovered in Papua, New Guinea in the early years of the last century, forbade divorce and fornication. They were wise enough to know that if they did not forbid it, they would destroy themselves. Missionary and Bible teacher Grahame Martin talks about this in his well-documented book *Headhunters.*[2]

According to John 8:34–36, Jesus insisted that He came to set believers free from sin and sinning. Romans 8:3–4 says that "God sending his own Son in the likeness of sinful flesh, and for sin, condemned sin in the flesh: That the righteousness of the law might be fulfilled in us, who walk not after the flesh, but after the Spirit." Christ's parable in Matthew 13:47–50 shows that His judgment is between the good and the bad.

A young friend of mine recently gave his heart to the Lord, but was soon taught in a church that a person is saved at the judgment purely on their faith, not because of their ways. Since he had been told that his faith had already eternally saved him, he felt justified in not changing his lifestyle. Even worse, he staggered his worldly friends by telling them that God does not judge people on their works, but on their faith. He left them in confusion by giving them the lie that you do not have to be good to get into heaven. Sadly, like a great majority, he had not been taught the difference between initial reconciliation and future eternal salvation.

My young friend should have been taught the warning of Ephesians 5:5, that nobody who practices sex outside of marriage or sinner or chaser after wealth has "any inheritance in the kingdom of Christ and of God." He should have received a number of instructions:

- Walk circumspectly [carefully], not as fools, but as wise" (Eph. 5:15).

- "Redeeming the time, because the days are evil" (Eph. 5:16).
- "Be ye not unwise, but understanding what the will of the Lord is" (Eph. 5:17).
- To stop his drinking bouts and instead "be filled with the [Holy] Spirit," in whom there is true joy that produces no hangovers (Eph. 5:18).
- To speak to himself "in psalms and hymns and spiritual songs, singing and making melody in [his] heart to the Lord" (Eph. 5:19).
- To give "thanks always for all things unto God and the Father in the name of our Lord Jesus Christ" (Eph. 5:20).
- We are to submit to each other as brothers and sisters in the fear of God (Eph. 5:21).
- Learning that real Christian wives submit to their husbands as to the Lord Himself and children to parents and teachers (Eph. 5:22, 6:1–3).
- A husband must love his wife "even as Christ also loved the church, and gave himself for it" (Eph. 5:25).
- His faith, without works of love, will avail nothing at his final judgment when the Lord comes back (Gal. 5:6; Titus 1:16).

It is interesting that God's revelation of His own character and His requirements for His people in the Old Testament agree completely with the teachings you are now reading in this book. Yet the content in this book is drawn from New Testament scriptures. It shows, as Hebrews 13:8 says, that Jesus Christ is the same yesterday, today, and *forever.*

…let the skies pour down righteousness: let the earth open, and let them bring forth salvation…together; I the Lord have created it.

—Isaiah 45:8

Chapter 9

FEAR GOD?

THE FOLLOWING IS taken from the writings of Dwight A. Pryor, the founder of the Center for Judaic–Christian Studies.[1]

> A Covenant is a mutual agreement with reciprocal obligations. A Covenant speaks therefore of mutuality and of corresponding commitments.
>
> *YHWH*, the unspoken Hebrew word for God, expects something of us. He requires complete loyalty and fidelity to the covenant. In biblical parlance, this is described as "walking" in His ways. It is walking in one's body in a way that is holy and set apart to Him. This type of covenantal language pervades the Torah and reflects the heart of Hebraic spirituality.

Consider these models of Godliness:

- "*Enoch* walked with God" (Genesis 5:24).
- "*Noah* walked with God" (Genesis 6:9). He was a a righteous and therefore blameless man.
- *Job* is described in Job 1:8 as a "blameless and upright man" and one who feared Yahweh (YHWH).
- *Abraham*, the father of our faith, received a call from God in Genesis 17:1: "I am Almighty God [*El Shaddai*]; walk before me and be blameless."

Fear of the Lord (*yir'at Adonai*) should be distinguished from the fear of divine punishment. The latter is a deterrent against sinning. Ultimately, however, fear of divine punishment is rooted in self-interest. Authentic *yir'at Adonnai*, however, is rooted in God's holiness. In other words, *fear of the Lord* connotes awe. This is not just any kind of awe, but awe accompanied by actions–reverence with results.

Yir'at Adonai is rooted in an awareness of the luminous divine radiance, the glory of His splendor, the unapproachable light of His presence, His very essence. It is a reverence for God and a deep respect for the sanctity of His name. It is an attitude accompanied and evidenced by works that are based not on our self-interest nor on fear but on the character of God Himself. Both types of fear were at work when the church began.

Acts 2:42–4 says, "And they continued steadfastly in the apostles' doctrine and fellowship, and in breaking of bread, and in prayers. And fear came upon every soul: and many wonders and signs were done by the apostles." This is not speaking about fear of God's judgments, but about rejoicing in God's awesomeness. Awe of God came on the early Jewish assembly because many signs and wonders were done through the apostles.

The terror of God's judgment, however, is recorded in Acts 5. The apostle *Shimon Petros* confronted Ananias, who sold a possession but lied about holding back some of the proceeds:

> Why hast thou conceived this thing in thine heart? thou hast not lied unto men, but unto God. And Ananias hearing these words fell down, and gave up the ghost: and great fear came on all them that heard these things.
>
> —ACTS 5:4–5

This was the fear of God's righteous and utterly holy judgment. God's holiness is unalterably opposed to every act of rebellion, wickedness, and evil (sinning). But the fear of God that Scripture enjoins is a summons to the awe of God and is accompanied by appropriate actions. We are expected by our judge to show our reverence by our works—our conduct.

Simon Peter, speaking to Cornelius, the first non-Jew to receive salvation, said, "Of a truth I perceive that God is no respecter of persons: But in every nation he that feareth him, and worketh righteousness [*tzedakah* or charity], is accepted with him [to be ready for conversion]" (Acts 10:34–35). Cornelius demonstrated his respect for God by his righteous works of giving alms to the needy.

Pryor concludes with this:

> The great Torah scholar S.R Hirsch in his commentary on the Psalms notes that "those who fear God have within themselves the awareness of God, and live their lives in constant realization of God and His will." It simply means that a righteous man walks sinlessly and does works of love (charity).[2]

To stand in awe of God is to have God continually before us and to walk in His ways. This was the heart of Old Testament spirituality. Fear of the Lord (*yir' at Adonai*) precedes and produces love for God. Responsive reverence was the very basis of faith and hope and trust in YHWH (Yahweh).

In Deuteronomy 10, Moses spoke to the people before they entered the Promised Land. He recapitulated all that God had commanded His covenant people and asked:

> And now, Israel, what doth the LORD thy God require of thee, but to fear the LORD thy God, to walk in all his ways, and to love him, and to serve the LORD thy God with all thy heart and with all thy soul, To keep the commandments of the LORD, and his statutes, which I command thee this day for thy good?
>
> —DEUTERONOMY 10:12–13

These are the details of what it means to fear the Lord:

- To walk in all His ways.
- To love Him.
- To serve the Lord your God with all your heart and all your soul.
- To keep the commands of the Lord.

In Deuteronomy 10:20, Moses adds, "You shall fear the Lord your God, Him alone shall you worship, and to Him shall you hold fast..." The fear of the Lord is related to our worship of God, and it involves clinging to or literally being glued to Him. Proverbs 1:7 teaches that the very beginning of wisdom is the fear of the Lord.

That concludes Dwight Pryor's commentary on the fear of God. It turns out to be a summary of what I have been teaching in this book. But this book centers around the new covenant. It becomes obvious that God's basic requirements for His people to obtain their future inheritance never change.

In John 1:29, John the Baptist proclaimed, "Behold the Lamb of God, which taketh away the sin of the world." When he announced the arrival of the Messiah whom all were awaiting, John proclaimed the good news that the prophecy of Daniel 9:24 was being fulfilled before their eyes. This was a prophecy that the Messiah would finish the transgression, make an end of sin, make atonement for iniquity, and bring in everlasting righteousness.

I believe that by the time we complete our thrilling excursion through Romans, chapters 6–8 we will never again doubt that Jesus of Nazareth fulfils all of the prophecy in Daniel 9:24. Our excursion starts very soon, in chapter 10.

The Bible tells us that a transgression is a breaking of Moses' Law! Jesus is the end of Moses' Law for righteousness. He has freed us from the curse of the Law. We are dead to the written Law and therefore freed from the transgression of it.

He also made an end of sins not mentioned in the Law. Romans 6:11 says that we are "dead indeed unto sin, but alive unto God through Jesus Christ our Lord." He Himself proclaimed that He frees us from slavery to sin. Anyone born of the Spirit of God cannot sin.

He made atonement for the iniquity we were all born with. Iniquity is "the law of sin," which forces all to commit sins. His sacrificial death atoned for all of our past sins, and His Spirit sets us free forever from the law of sin, which was unbeatable before Christ.

He ushered in the age of righteousness. We were once the slaves of sin, but now we have become the slaves of righteousness. And He is able to keep us from falling. We obey all of God's laws when we walk in the Spirit by faith.

Alleluia! The Messiah has come. Jesus has fulfilled Daniel's prophecy. All the things promised in Daniel 9:24 need to become a reality in our lives if we are to obtain our eternal salvation on Judgment Day. Otherwise, Jesus our Messiah will say, I do not know you!

Restoring Righteousness

> I have made the earth, and created man upon it...I have raised him up in righteousness, and I will direct all his ways: he shall build my city, and he shall let go my captives, not for price nor reward, saith the Lord of hosts.
>
> —Isaiah 45:12–13

Part II

Our Life-Changing Excursion

THIS SECOND PART of my book is a verse-by-verse explanation of chapters six, seven, and part of eight of Paul's letter to the Romans. These verses are the nucleus of everything I have written in this book. Indeed, they are the heart, the very core of all that is written in the New Testament. Luke records what our Lord Jesus said about His apostle Paul in Acts 9:15–16:

> He is a chosen vessel unto me [Jesus], to bear my name before the Gentiles, and kings, and the children of Israel: For I will shew him how great things he must suffer for my name's sake.

Chapter 10

Why Did I Have to Die?

The apostle Paul's dissertation on sin and sinning in Romans 6, 7, and 8 is the benchmark for this book. In Romans 6:1, Paul writes:

> Shall we continue in sin, that grace may abound?

For nearly two thousand years the church has generally answered this question with a resounding "Yes, we are all continuing sinners saved by grace." However Paul's response in the very next verse is a resounding "No, never let it be said!"

Yet, it is generally accepted that every recognized Christian denomination is unified in the belief that Christians will sin until the day they die. Many claim that their sinning gives glory to God because they imagine that God by His grace continually forgives them. A common bumper sticker says it this way: "Christians are not perfect... just forgiven!"

Are we trying to fool ourselves into believing that our sinning serves to highlight God's grace? Paul must have foreseen this foolish theory when he penned verse 1 of Romans 6.

It appears, almost incredibly, that most church doctrines flatly contradict many of the teachings and most of the warnings the apostles Paul, John, and Peter gave against sinning. Perhaps you are thinking, *I do not really know what my church teaches in this area.* Well, there is a very easy and simple way to find out.

Go to your leader and ask, "Can I stop sinning before I die?" Paul carefully lays out the scriptural answer to that question:

Romans 6:2

> God forbid. How shall we, that are dead to sin, live any longer therein?

Putting that in today's English, Paul is saying, "Don't let God ever hear you say that your sinning highlights God's mercy and grace. It is a lie! For you are dead, and dead men do not commit sin."

You may ask how being dead and buried relates to no longer being a sinner? Paul, by the Spirit of God, carefully answers this important question in the next ten verses of Romans 6.

At this point I want you to remember that dead mankind is very different from angels, who can commit sins. The New Testament clearly states that at death, man is set free from sin, the old slave master that, in life, had forced him to commit sins even against his own will. Psalm 51:5, states that mankind is enslaved to sin from conception. However, Romans 6:7 says, "For he that is dead is freed from sin." 1 Peter 4.1 adds, "He that hath suffered [death] in the flesh hath ceased from sin."

The Lord Jesus and His apostle Paul, after whom He taught, was glorified are, I believe, the first two in the Bible to explain that sin is a master that lives in our flesh. It is vital knowledge for us if we expect to be the spotless bride of Christ at His coming.

To understand Romans chapters 6–8, we need to know that the word *sin* usually does not mean "sinning." *Sin* mostly refers to a slave master that came from Satan to Adam and from Adam to all mankind down through the centuries. Jesus Christ descended from heaven as God in flesh to "[take] away the sin of the world" (John 1:29).

In John 11:26, Jesus said that whoever believes in Him will never die spiritually. But our bodies have to die, not because of the sins we have committed, but because our bodies are where the slave master—sin—lives.

Sin, like an irreversible disease, lives in my flesh from my conception. But once I die, sin, like all disease, has lost its power over me.

The blood of Christ is for the forgiveness of sins committed. It reconciles us to God.

However, it is only by our *own death* that we are set free from sin. This is a Bible truth. Sin cannot die; we die to sin!

Most religious philosophies recognize that the lusts of the flesh must be overcome if evil is to be defeated. Therefore, they teach: beat your body, sleep on the floor or on nails, fast, abstain from certain foods, wear plain clothes, cover the flesh from head to toe, deny yourself all pleasure, do not marry, wear shirts made of hair, live in seclusion, and so on. But all these attempts to die to the flesh are of no value in overcoming sin. Has anyone ever claimed that their efforts set them completely free from sin's power? No!

They may beat one lust, but another will replace it.

Man has a saying, "If you are human, you will commit sins." This agrees with Romans 3:23, which says, "For all have sinned, and come short of the glory of God."

But Jesus came to change mankind from being sinners. He said:

> Whosoever committeth sin is the servant of sin...If the Son therefore shall make you free, ye shall be free indeed.
>
> —John 8:34, 36

This is a promise from God to man via His Son. Jesus came to set us humans free from being slaves to sin. It is a life changer—a lifesaver!

In the main, we have rejected the truth that Christ has set us free from our slave master. We shy away from faith in the hard-to-understand promises.

Human reasoning is faith's greatest enemy and doubt's greatest ally.

Romans 6:3

> Know ye not, that so many of us as were baptized into Jesus Christ were baptized into his death?

Dear Christian, Paul is now taking us into the realms of faith, from the seen to the unseen. Underlining all his teaching is the truth: that "without faith it is impossible to please [God]" (Heb. 11:6). The promise of Romans 1:17 helps us realize that we gain entry into Christ's life through faith in Him. We were with Him when He spoke the words "Let there be light" (Gen. 1:3). Romans 6:5 teaches, "We have been planted together in the likeness of his death, [and] we shall be also in the likeness of his resurrection." If we are in Christ, we are seated with Him in heavenly places, according to Ephesians 1:20.

All of our thoughts, words, and actions are Christ's by His Spirit if we will truly believe it and confess it. Romans 8:2 calls this the way of the Spirit of life in Christ Jesus.

Paul is asking, "Have you forgotten or were you not instructed before your water baptism that in baptism you entered into Christ's death? You died with Him."

Please notice that Paul is not saying here that Christ died for us, but that we died in His death. We hung on that cross, and we died. We felt no pain because, as Hebrews 2:9 says, He tasted death for us. It is our "faith death."

Yes, it is true that we cannot stop sinning until after we die. This is the reason Jesus took us to death in His death.

We cannot make any real progress in overcoming sin until we accept in faith that we died on the cross with Jesus. We cannot understand this, and that is why we need faith. We do not need faith if we can understand or see something. In faith we accept that our past sins were all forgiven at the cross. In faith we accept that we died with Him on the cross.

Paul is not just teaching us an optional extra. It is the key to our eternal salvation in the kingdom of Jesus Christ. Satan does not want us to believe that our carnal man is dead. As 1 John 3:8 teaches, everyone who sins is of the devil.

In Mark 8:34, Jesus said that we must deny ourselves and take up our cross if we want to follow Him. The cross is a sign of suffering and death. In Romans 6, Paul reminds us that we were taken to death with Christ at Golgotha. We are called to carry the cross as a continual reminder that our old (carnal) man is dead and buried.

But self demands that we try to die every day. Self rejects God's promises, and it is not into faith. Instead, it wants to do things "my way" and delights in actions which require sound and sensible reasoning. Philosophical religions advise their followers to die daily to self. But Christ says you are already dead, and dead men are already freed from sin. We receive it by faith.

If our carnal self is already dead, why do we need to try to die daily? We may say with the apostle Paul in 1 Corinthians 15:31, "I die daily." Yes, but he was talking figuratively about the fact that he was continually under threat of death by persecution, which he described in 1 Corinthians 15:30–34. There is no way that we can interpret this statement of Paul's to mean dying to self. If anyone knew that he was already dead, it was Paul. He taught us: "I am crucified with Christ... and the life which I now live in the flesh I live by the faith of the Son of God, who loved me, and gave himself for me" (Gal. 2:20).

Going under the waters of baptism signifies that our old man is dead and buried. God's principle is that new life has to be preceded by the death of the old. Take a look at the life cycle of a butterfly or a plant.

For this reason, Jesus our Savior took us to death; so that we could have new life. I had to die to get new life, and thanks be to God, I have entered into my past death at water baptism.

Christ's death on the cross is not only a sacrifice of atonement. It included the death of every carnal man in Him. With the belief and confession that I died in Christ's death, I am ready for the next benefit of my believer's baptism—His new life in me!

Romans 6:4

> Therefore we are buried with him by baptism into death: that like as Christ was raised up from the dead by the glory of the Father, even so we also should walk in newness of life.

Going down in the waters of baptism is an action that is like burying a dead person. Paul is teaching us that not only did we die with Christ, but we also shared His burial in the tomb. Burial is for the dead. The tomb is not for the living.

But just as Christ was raised from the dead to be a spiritual man, we now share in His new life. It is surely time for us to realize that our Redeemer came not just to bring forgiveness and reconciliation, but to give us a new life. He provided believers with the sinless life of the risen and glorified Jesus, our Christ.

Does our eternal salvation depend on it? Yes it does!

Romans 5.10 states, "We shall be saved by his life." Galatians 2.20 adds, "I live; yet not I, but Christ liveth in me."

How do we live this life of Christ? We do it by faith. We believe it and confess it. Can you see how impossible it is to live the life of Christ if we go around thinking and saying, "I will go on sinning till I die" or "I have to try to die daily"?

In John 12:24, Jesus states: "Verily, verily, I say unto you, Except a corn of wheat fall into the ground and die, it abideth alone: but if it die, it bringeth forth much fruit."

In Ephesians 4:24, the apostle Paul says, "And... put on the new man, which after God is created in righteousness [sinlessness] and true holiness." The phrase *put on* means to grasp it by faith.

Romans 6:5

> For if we have been planted together in the likeness of his death, we shall be also in the likeness of his resurrection:

Christ was resurrected with a new body—an indestructible spiritual body, an eternal body. First Corinthians 15:50 teaches that "flesh and blood cannot inherit the kingdom of God." Christians who died blameless will each receive a spiritual body on resurrection day. Immediately following them, the Christians who are yet on earth and are living a holy and blameless lifestyle will be changed "in the twinkling of an eye" (1 Cor. 15:52). They will rise to join their brothers and sisters and so be with their dear Lord in the clouds. Our spiritual body will not be able to be tempted to commit sin. It will be indestructible and ageless. It will be glorious, as described in 1 Corinthians 15:20, 42–58 and 1 Thessalonians 4:7, 14–17.

By faith in God's promise we are able, in this life on earth, to have the likeness of Christ's resurrection life. His resurrection life becomes our lifestyle when we walk in the promise that it is no longer we who live but Christ who lives in us. We are a new creation. We walk in it by believing it and confessing it.

In such a way, we come out of the kingdom of darkness "into the kingdom of his dear Son" (Col. 1:13). Believe it, confess it, and do it. As 1 Peter 1:4 and 11 promise, we will thereby receive our inheritance of an earthly sinless life and a future eternal life in the kingdom of Jesus Christ.

If we are prepared to walk in these promises, we will be impervious to temptation to commit sin. Jesus Christ will be living in us by His Spirit.

We will rejoice that the way of the Spirit of life in Christ Jesus has set us free from the law of sin. I rejoice every day in this new life, freed from sin and sinning. I believe and I obey, according to Romans 8:2 and 4.

Genesis 2:16–3:24 tells how Adam disobeyed God, Eve disobeyed her husband, and they lost paradise. In 1 Samuel 15:22, the prophet Samuel told King Saul that obedience is better than sacrifice. Verse 26 goes on to tell how God "rejected [Saul] from being king over Israel" because he did not obey His instructions to totally destroy the Amalekites. Instead, he had saved some sheep and oxen from the Amalekites to offer as a sacrifice to God.

Will you, dear Reader, obey God's promise of your past death and your new life in the Spirit? According to Romans 8:1–2, it is the only way that we will avoid condemnation at judgment.

Romans 6:6

> *Knowing this,* that our old man is crucified with him, that the body of sin might be destroyed, that henceforth we should not serve sin.

Is Paul repeating himself? Yes! He knows this is hard, and he wants to stress that his teaching is a matter of eternal life or eternal death to a Christian. He wants us to get verse 6 right, even if everyone else has it wrong.

Know it, says Paul. He means that we do not just agree with what we read but that we take it to heart. We must accept that it is a challenge and that it is about our eternal life.

Know it inside out. If we do not know perfectly what Paul is teaching in verse 6, Christ died in vain and we will continue in vanity. The reality of verse 6 is something that the Holy Spirit reveals to those whom He fills. It is written in the New Testament, but often His revelation is drowned out by the voice of teachers who mislead many saints. They do not fully understand Romans 6, and especially verse 6. The truth is snatched away as birds eat up seeds before they have time to germinate.

Know verse 6 when temptations come. We need to know it as we work, when we play, when we eat, lying in bed, when we study, and when we are asleep. We need to know it in church, on our mountaintops, or in our valleys.

Please do not continue reading this book until you have grasped verse 6, eaten it, digested it, and tasted the sweetness of its satisfaction. Its end is life eternal.

My old carnal man, who was ruled by sin, has died. He died on the cross with Christ. Each day, I personally carry in my mind a picture of myself dead on the cross.

With the original body of flesh destroyed, sin can no longer rule us. It can never again force us to commit sins against our will.

In Romans 7:18–19, Paul is emphatic that the old man is unable to resist sin by willpower. If we could resist temptation to commit sin with righteousness that comes by keeping the law, "then Christ is dead in vain" (Gal. 2:21). Sin, the slave master, cannot control a dead man (a corpse). Sin is not dead on the cross; my old body of flesh is dead.

Say it with me: *Sin is not dead on the cross; the slave is dead—set free from sin's control.* Yes, as John 8:36 says, "If the

Son therefore shall make you free [from sin's control], ye shall be free indeed."

Jesus says it. Paul says it. Peter says it. I believe it.

The apostle John says: "Anyone who says or thinks that he [his old man] was not a sinner makes God and himself a liar."

It may take us some time to come to terms with the truth of Romans 6—that we were crucified and died. Christians of long standing will have to overcome a strong and contrary mind-set.

We have been under the impression that we will never be free from sinning. Now God comes along and says that he whom the Son sets free [by death] is freed indeed.

I have found that knowledge—especially heart knowledge—is built up brick by brick from a solid foundation. That foundation is Christ. We cannot skip a brick. Do not skip the knowledge of Romans 6:6. John teaches, "Whosoever is born of God…cannot sin, because he is born of God" (1 John 3:9). He confirms Paul's teaching that dead men cannot continue to sin.

Never forgetting that I died with Christ, I can now add another brick—verse 7.

Romans 6:7

> He that is dead is freed from sin.

So our freedom starts when we accept our death with Christ at His crucifixion, for sin has no power over dead flesh.

Everyone should already understand that disease has no power over dead flesh and that Law has no power over dead flesh. It should be obvious that those bodies (skeletons) in the graveyard cannot sin. All their flesh has been, or is being, destroyed until only hair and bones remain. Verse seven is telling me that my soul and spirit cannot sin after it has left my dead body.

In his letter to the Colossian church, Paul says, "For ye are dead, and your life is hid with Christ in God" (Col. 3:3). A

Christian should know that he is a living dead man, that he should no longer serve sin.

Paul told the Galatian church: "I am crucified with Christ: nevertheless I live; yet not I, but Christ liveth in me: and the life which I now live in the flesh I live by the faith of the Son of God…" (Gal. 2:20).

Worldly philosophies recognize that man has an evil nature. But Jesus took that evil-natured man to death on His cross.

Why not accept your past death? Confess it every morning. *I died with Jesus, and a dead person cannot sin.*

We know nothing of the agony of that death, for, as Hebrews 2:9 explains, Jesus tasted the pain for us. We need faith in the unseen to accept that our natural man is dead. It is a New Testament promise. It is Bible. It is God's Word. Are God's promises true?

We did not have to die at Calvary for the sins we committed. Jesus Christ's death atoned for them. No, we had to die because we were born with sin—an unseen master of evil—which forced us to be sinners.

Sin was our pharaoh. But this pharaoh has no hold over the dead; they are beyond his control. Death brings freedom to a slave.

> My righteousness is near; my salvation is gone forth, and mine arms shall judge the people; the isles shall wait upon me, and on mine arm shall they trust.
>
> —Isaiah 51:5

Chapter 11

Life after Death

Romans 6:8 says:

> Now if we be dead with Christ, we believe that we shall also live with him.

We accepted our death *by faith,* but we can also now share in His life by faith. By receiving the gift of His Spirit, we can begin to experience eternal life, for the Spirit gives life. We were forgiven by the spilling of His blood, but, according to Romans 5:10, we are *saved by His life working in us.*

Eternal salvation is awarded to those who have lived a lifestyle ruled by Christ, as described in Galatians 2:20. It is received only after a converted lifetime of walking by faith in the Spirit of life in Christ Jesus, so clearly expressed in Romans 8:2 and 4. In Romans 1:17, we learn that it is a day-to-day faith walk. Romans 2:7 and Hebrews 3:14 teach that we must live it and persevere.

Hebrews 2:2–3 and 4:6 and 11 present eternal salvation as a lifestyle of obedience. My eternal salvation is by His life reigning in me. Jesus is the One who gives me the gift of the person of the Holy Spirit. He is the Spirit of God, the Spirit of our heavenly Father, and the Spirit of Jesus our Lord. He is the promise of the Father. He is the Spirit of grace. He is a Person, and He is God. The instant that Jesus decides to give us the Holy Spirit is the time when we start to live our new life. It is His life in us. He is eternal life.

We become "Christ-men" by walking in His Spirit. The natural man, who was ruled by sin, is dead!

Satan never had any power to force us to commit sins; neither had mankind nor our own flesh. Sin—and sin alone—forced us to commit sins, even against our own will.

But praise the Lord, we died and accepted our death by faith. Now sin has no more power over us, and our new life is by our faith in the risen Christ. He lives in us by His Spirit of glory and truth. We are Christ–men, and, as 1 John 3:9 teaches, Christ–men cannot commit sins.

Romans 6:9

> Knowing that Christ being raised from the dead dieth no more; death hath no more dominion over him.

First Corinthians 15:42–50 explains that a resurrected body is spiritual, and it cannot die. Jesus was the first man among many brothers to receive a spiritual immaterial body which cannot die.

Sin cannot live in a spiritual body. With resurrection, a man is freed forever from sin. It will then be no longer necessary for him to live by faith in his death with Christ on the cross.

Sin is punished by death. Where there is no sin, there is no death. Romans 6:23 says that "the wages of sin [is] death."

The Bible assures us that there is a second death for convicted sinners on Judgment Day:

> I saw the souls of them that were beheaded for the witness of Jesus, and for the word of God, and which had not worshipped the beast, neither his image, neither had received his mark upon their foreheads, or in their hands; and they lived and reigned with Christ... But the rest of the dead lived not again [were not resurrected]... This is the first resurrection. [It is also called the resurrection of the just.] Blessed and holy is he that hath part in the first resurrection: on such the second death hath no power.
>
> —Revelation 20:4–6

The second resurrection comes later:

> And I saw a great white throne, and him that sat on it, from whose face the earth and the heaven fled away... And I saw the dead, small and great, stand before God; and the books were opened: and another book was opened, which is the book of life: and the dead were judged out of those things which were written in the books, according to their works... And death and hell were cast into the lake of fire. *This is the second death.* [Eternity in fire!] And whosoever was not found written in the book of life was cast into the lake of fire.
>
> —Revelation 20:11–15

Righteous souls do not go to a second death for they have eternal life. The second death is a living death for all eternity in the lake of fire.

Romans 6:9 says, "Knowing that Christ being raised from the dead dieth no more; death hath no more dominion over him."

This is also true for those who in Christ are kept blameless till they die. They will not be cast into the lake of fire, which is the second death. Just as death has no more dominion over Christ, it will have no more dominion over them.

Romans 6:10

> For in that he died, he died unto sin once: but in that he liveth, he liveth unto God.

Jesus Christ our Lord was a man like us in all things except sin. Hebrews 4:15 teaches that He was tempted to commit sins. Yet, He did not have that slave master called sin living in His body of flesh, for His Father was not a man, but God.

He laid down His life for the sins we committed. He did it for everybody born into this world—past, present, and future. He also took their bodies, which contained sin, their slave master, to death with Himself.

Christ also took up His new spiritual body and returned in it to His Father in heaven. Now He is seated back in the glory from which He came to earth. The Word who became flesh—the second person in the Godhead—has been appointed King of kings and Lord of lords. Also, according to Romans 8:29, He is the firstborn of many brothers who will be born again of the Spirit of God. Since we enter by faith into Christ's life—past, present, and future—we are also seated with Him at His Father's right hand on the throne of God in heaven.

Christ will return on Judgment Day. First Peter 1:17 tells how every man has to be judged by Jesus Christ, for God does not favor any man. The blameless, holy, and righteous ones who have walked obediently in Him in this life will inherit their eternal life in heaven. Sinners will be sent to the lake of fire.

Hebrews 12:14 says that no man will see God without holiness. We must get rid of a mind-set that thinks, *I will never be blameless and holy*. That is an insult to Christ's successful work and an insult to the Spirit of grace who brings us eternal life. Christ's life in us will enable us to stay sinless—righteous, blameless, and holy—for we are, as Romans 5:10 declares, *"saved by His life."*

Dear Reader, as we move through Romans 6, please keep in mind that the great apostle Paul is teaching something new. His aim is to reveal to us that sin is a tyrant who lives in the living flesh of man from conception. In Romans 7, he expands the teaching to show that sin forces us to commit sins even against our strongest will. We can overcome it only by our "death of faith" in Jesus Christ.

Paul was trying to teach this doctrine to people who had a mind-set that we can overcome sin by the Law or self-denial and willpower. These people, right down to these last days, conclude that they are fighting a losing battle with sin. They believe that they are stuck with it until death. They are right about that. But they do not know—or will not— accept the good news that they have already died with Christ.

Once again I am blowing the whistle on those who still believe they are stuck with sin. The whistle says, "Time's up, the game is over!"

Romans 6:11

> Likewise reckon ye also yourselves to be dead indeed unto sin, but alive unto God through Jesus Christ our Lord.

The name *Christ Jesus our Lord* means that the man called Jesus of Galilee is our Savior and our God. Colossians 1:16 tells us that all things, seen and unseen, were created through Him. He is the Messiah promised by all the prophets of the Old Testament.

By our absolute trust in Him, we are in Christ. And by His Spirit, He lives in us. Therefore we can be certain that we too died with Him and are dead to sin. But we also came up from the waters of baptism and are sharing in His resurrection life. We are now alive to God.

The word *to reckon* is special. It has the same meaning as the business reckoning we receive on a receipt at the supermarket checkout. The printout shows the cost price of every item purchased and the total amount spent. It is called in the business world "a reckoning." It is the finalized, indisputable record of a transaction for both the buyer and the seller.

In the same way, the Holy Spirit says, "Reckon yourself dead to sin." Christ sees us as carnally dead. He reckons us dead. What is our problem?

It is an indisputable truth. It is God's word. It is sealed in our lives when we believe it and confess it. Say it and believe it: *I died on the cross with Christ, and I am dead to sin.*

Our death is behind us, and now we are free to go on and reckon ourselves alive to God through Christ Jesus. Every day I reckon that I am a new man, a new creation who walks by faith in the indwelling Spirit of Jesus Christ. Sin has no more hold on me. I am freed. It's Bible! No born-of-the-Spirit Christian should dispute it or doubt it.

When the devil hears us confessing our belief in Romans 6:11, he packs up and leaves. He knows that he is wasting his time when he tempts us to commit sins. He will come back at a later date to try us, to see if we have any doubts of Christ's promise. We need to persevere in faith and keep our body under, as 1 Corinthians 9:27 says.

We have been freed from the power of sin, and we must now keep it locked out. Adam and Eve were originally free from the power of sin, but they foolishly opened the door when they heard it's persuasive call.

I have found that temptations disappear like dirty water down the sink as soon as I declare, "I am dead to sin and alive to God in Christ Jesus." Try it; it works. It must work because, as John 3:21 and 8:12 show, the light of truth makes darkness flee. When anybody tells us that we are still sinning, we can reply kindly but firmly, "I am dead to sin and alive to God in Christ Jesus, according to the Bible!"

The only reason we will not be castaways on our judgment day is if we have lived a sinless life in Christ's imparted power since we were born of the Spirit of God. This power is described in Romans 8:1–2 and 4. Walking a sinless lifestyle simply means that nothing we *do* displeases Jesus Christ our Lord. Hebrews 11:6 says we cannot please Him without faith.

The Holy Spirit spoke in my ear as I lay in the stillness of dawn one morning and said, "All doubt is sin." It took me some months of pondering these words and searching the Scriptures to see that He was speaking about my whole way of life. Is my lifestyle centered on gladly accepting that everything is going to work for good in my life because I love God?

I was reminded too of the divine truth that love believes all things. How much am I trusting God or my fellow man or even my brothers and sisters in the Lord? Do I believe everything anyone says until it is proved wrong, or am I a suspicious doubter of God and man?

Some of you may already doubt that all doubt is sin. If that is true, start inquiring about it. Honest inquiry is not doubt. Doubt is *unwarranted* unbelief. I have taken a long look at Romans 14:23, which declares that "whatsoever [is] not of faith is sin." It means that anything I do—thinking it may be sinful—is a sin, whether it is or is not in God's will.

In another vein, I thought about the English law, which declares a man to be innocent until proven guilty. In today's world, it is so easy to become suspicious, distrustful, and even cynical of everyone and everything. I share these words that the Holy Spirit occasionally gives me so that you too may chew on them. They are what I call life changers and lifesavers.

The apostle Peter warns about our judge, "who without respect of persons [whether I am a Christian or not a Christian] judgeth according to every man's work [the deeds I do in this life on earth]..." In 1 Peter 1:17, He tells us to "pass the time of [our] sojourning here in fear."

Therefore, I am going to walk without sinning every day of my new life, and so I will be saved from God's wrath, which sends sinners to the lake of fire. I have no intention of mocking God by being on the treadmill of sin-and-repent, sin-and-repent until I die! It is my responsibility to walk in Christ's love in the Holy Spirit, in the knowledge available to me from the Bible and from God's creation.

I cannot use false and flattering teachings as my excuse for failure. Nobody but myself is accountable to Christ my judge. I do not intend to insult the Spirit of grace by continuing to commit sins, as Hebrews 10:26–30 warns against. In Matthew 12:32, Jesus taught that insulting the Spirit of grace, the Holy Spirit, is an unforgivable sin.

Charles Finney (1792–1875) taught "not to expect to live without sin through Christ is unbelief."[1] I agree!

> Lift up your eyes to the heavens, and look upon the earth beneath: for the heavens shall vanish away like smoke, and the earth shall wax old like a garment, and they that dwell therein shall die in like manner: but my salvation shall be for ever, and my righteousness shall not be abolished.
>
> —Isaiah 51:6

Chapter 12

Bolt the Door and Windows

ROMANS 6:12 SAYS:

> Therefore do not let sin reign in your mortal body that you should obey it in the lusts thereof.

Paul is saying, "Do not open the door to ever sin again." Sin is a dictator that will settle for nothing less than to reign over us. Lust is a God-given desire that is perverted by sin to force us to commit a sin.

Man is attracted to woman for the purpose of marriage and children. Sin perverts this into lustful desires, acts of sex outside of marriage, adultery, pornography, prostitution, homosexuality, and the like.

Mankind is given a healthy appetite for food and drink. Sin perverts it into desires and acts of gluttony and intoxication.

Sin turns normal and healthy desires into sinning desires and acts. The Bible calls them lusts.

God has given mankind a healthy desire for knowledge in general, but not for the knowledge of good and evil. Sin says that the knowledge of good and evil is indispensable. Sin lusts after the knowledge of good and evil for mankind because it is the power of sin.

Sin turns God-given desires into thoughts ands actions that break God's unwritten law of love. Colossians 3:1–3 counsels us:

> If ye then be risen with Christ, seek those things which are above, where Christ sitteth on the right hand of God. Set your affection on things above, not on things on the earth. For ye are dead, and your life is hid with Christ in God.

Reach for the stars. Romans 8:4–6 instructs us to walk in the Spirit and not satisfy the sinful desires of our body of flesh.

We have been set free, but we must make sure that we stay that way. We do it by cooperating with Christ in us, His faith working through His love. In obeying the Spirit of Christ Jesus, we are assured that sin will never again reign over us. We are to be eternally saved by His life working in us, as Romans 5:10 promises.

By His Spirit, Christ is in us—our only hope of glory! We cannot get there alone. Acts 4:12 declares that there is no other name under heaven whereby a man can be saved.

Romans 6:13

> Neither yield ye your members as instruments of unrighteousness unto sin: but yield yourselves unto God, as those that are alive from the dead, and your members [as] instruments of righteousness unto God.

Please notice that *un*righteousness means sinning. Sin is still alive, but our old man of flesh is dead. Sin has no hold over us so we do not let it entice us to listen to or obey its call.

I am one who is alive from the dead. I would be a fool to be tricked into yielding my body members to commit sin. However, I am not a fool, for I yield my members to do the work of righteousness. I obey the Spirit. My body members—my eyes, ears, nose, mouth, tongue, brain, arms, legs, hands, private parts, lungs, stomach, feet, toes, and fingers—are the individual parts of my body. Satan, through sin, wants me to use my members to commit sins. But I refuse to go back to the bondage of sin. I walk in righteousness by obeying the Spirit of God.

I am a Christ-man! Jesus bought me back from sin, not with gold and silver, but with His blood.

Even though I still have an earthen body, it is no longer filled with water. Instead, it is filled with wine. I am a vessel filled with the person of the Spirit of Christ Jesus. My Beloved is mine, and I am His. I live by His direction. He is my Lord, not any man or other spirit.

Ezekiel 3:20–21 defines righteousness as being sinless. First John 5:17 says, "All unrighteousness is sin." If we are to receive our eternal inheritance, God rightly requires that we put on the new man, who is created in holiness and true righteousness. We are required by God to live a righteous, sinless life. Otherwise how could He trust us in heaven?

My life is hidden in Christ, but it is not hidden from Christ. One day, Christ will be our last judge, and He will judge us on what we have done since we were born of God. We must please God. Second Corinthians 5:10 says:

> For we must all appear before the judgment seat of Christ; that every one may receive the things done in his body, according to that he hath done, whether it be good or bad.

Philippians 2:12–13 adds:

> ...work out your own salvation with fear and trembling. For it is God which worketh in you both to will and to do of his good pleasure.

Paul writes of himself:

> I count all things...but dung [*excreta*], that I may win Christ, and be found in him, not having mine own [self-righteousness], which is of the law, but that which is through [obeying Christ Jesus by faith], the righteousness [sinlessness] which is of God by faith [in Christ and His promises].
>
> —PHILIPPIANS 3:8–9

> If by any means I might attain unto the resurrection of the dead. Not as though I had already attained [to being resurrected from the dead—eternally saved]...but I follow after [it, *hoping*] that I may apprehend that...[which Christ has called me to].
>
> —PHILIPPIANS 3:11–12

When I preached the same message in the streets of Jerusalem my friends left me for they knew that stoning could follow.

Paul makes it even clearer that we must hope for our eternal salvation. In Romans 8:23–24, he says that we are "waiting for the adoption, to wit, the redemption of our body. For we are saved by hope..." He explains that we hope for what we do not see and we wait for it with patience.

In his letter to the Colossian church, Paul writes:

> You were circumcised with the circumcision of Christ by death to your flesh and co buried with Him in Baptism, in whom you were also co raised by faith in the operation of God who raised Him from the dead.
>
> —COLOSSIANS 2:12–13, *NESTLE'S GREEK TEXT*

> [Christ has reconciled you to God] in order to present you Holy and blameless and irreproachable if you continue to walk by faith in him and his promises which is the good news.
>
> —COLOSSIANS 1:22–23, *NESTLE'S GREEK TEXT*

It is apparent from the New Testament that Jesus will not be able to present us to His Father in heaven if we are not holy, blameless, and irreproachable in our daily life. If our lifestyle is not blameless, it brings disgrace to the name of Christ. It discredits Him among men and insults the Holy Spirit of grace. God has called us and equipped us to be overcomers of sin and sinning, as we saw in our discussion of Revelation, chapters 2 and 3, earlier in this book. Our part is to cooperate and do it by a confessing faith.

Born-of-the-Spirit Christians are just as free from the power of sin as Adam was before he allowed himself to be deceived:

ROMANS 6:14

> For sin shall not have dominion over you: for ye are not under the law, but under grace.

The root meaning of *grace* is "a gift." Our gift comes to us from our Father, through Christ, by the Holy Spirit—the Spirit of grace. Our gift is the ongoing new and eternal life of Jesus Christ, which follows the gift of our death with Christ.

Because we are no longer under the Law of the old covenant, we do not have a list of what is good and what is evil. We have something better. We have the life of Christ guiding us, not by example but by direction. We hear a voice behind us saying, "This is the way, walk ye in it" (Isa. 30:21). Christ has redeemed us from the frustration of trying to live righteously by written laws.

The definition of *sin* is "to break one of God's laws." This is why the Scripture says that sin gets its power from the Law.

Since we are not under the Law but under the life of Christ, it follows that sin has no control over us. Without the Law, sin is as good as dead.

We, like our original parents, can now walk righteously through the fellowship and guidance of God alone. They began under God's grace, trusting in Him alone to lead them on the path of righteousness. They fell when Eve disobeyed God and Adam obeyed his wife. The only way we can fall is to disobey the leading of Christ by His indwelling shepherd, the Spirit of truth.

A born-of-the-Spirit Christian does not receive a law engraved by the finger of God on stone tablets. Instead, he receives the indwelling lawgiver Himself, the Holy Spirit.

> For what the law could not do, in that it was weak through the flesh, God sending his own Son in the likeness of sinful flesh, and for sin, condemned sin in the flesh.
>
> —ROMANS 8:3

We disobey Christ and His new covenant if we go back to the commandments as our way of life. Using the Ten Commandments as our guide to life instead of faith in Christ will immediately put us under sin, our old slave master. We will be under another law, the law of sin. We will be back on the road to the lake of fire. Trying to mix the Law and faith is worse still. Jesus told the church of the Laodiceans that He was very displeased because they were "neither cold nor hot." He said, "So then because thou art lukewarm, and neither cold nor hot, I will spue thee out of my mouth" (Rev. 3:15–16).

I am sorry to say that I have seen and read of a great number of Spirit-filled Christians who are returning to the Law. It is a disaster because, as 2 Corinthians 3:6 shows, "The letter killeth."

Christians are right when they declare that they will go on sinning till they die. But as we know from Romans 6:6, we died with Christ and have already finished with sin and are now alive to God. All achieved by believing it and confessing it. What a terrible thing it is to die in our sins! In Mark 9:47, Jesus says it is better for us to pluck out our eyes than be sent to hell if our eyes are causing us to commit sin.

If we return to the Law, we resurrect the carnal man. He is under the dominion of sin, and, as Romans 6:23 teaches, "The wages of sin is death."

If righteousness could come by the Ten Commandments, then, as Galatians 2:21 says, Christ died in vain. However, righteousness was *imputed* to man by the grace of Christ's death, and it was *imparted* to man by the grace of Christ's (Resurrection) life.

I have noticed that many professing Christians show by their conduct that they won't do anything to lose the good opinion of men. They refuse to accept the persecution that they must encounter if they give themselves up to root out sin from the world and the church.

> Then said the Lord unto me; This gate shall be shut, it shall not be opened, and no man shall enter in by it; because *the Lord . . . hath entered in by it, therefore it shall be shut*
>
> —Ezekiel 44:2

Chapter 13

Don't Swallow Camels

ROMANS 6:15 SAYS:

> What then? shall we sin, because we are not under the law, but under grace? God forbid.

Paul is posing the question, "Do you think it is right to tolerate sinning because we are in a covenant of God's grace?" No! Never! God, through Paul, forbids the false teaching that tolerates sin because of grace and that says we are saints, and at the same time sinners. If we swallow the camel that says we are both saint and sinner, we will surely die.

Common sense tells us that we mock God, reject Christ's victory, and insult the Spirit of grace if we use His grace as a covering for a lifestyle of sinning. God pours out His grace so that we *can* walk righteously without breaking God's law.

Paul told the Ephesian church: "For by grace are ye saved [reconciled] through faith...the gift of God...[to do] good works" (Eph. 2:8, 10). He says that even faith comes through God's grace.

We are saved (reconciled) so that we can do His works. *Our eternal salvation is by these works of God, works that we do.* Second Peter 1:9–11 teaches:

> But he that lacketh these things is blind, and cannot see afar off, and hath forgotten that he was purged from his old sins. Wherefore the rather, brethren, give diligence to make your calling and election sure: for if ye do these things, ye shall never fall: For so an entrance shall be ministered unto you abundantly into the everlasting kingdom of our Lord and Saviour Jesus Christ.

The good works of God do not follow as automatically as some teach. No! They follow on from day-to-day obedience to the leading of the Holy Spirit.

We cannot be saved to continue sinning; that is a contradiction of terms. Revelation 19:7–8 tells about the marriage supper of the Lamb, which will celebrate the eternal salvation of the bride who has prepared herself with good works of righteousness.

Romans 6:16

> Know ye not, that to whom ye yield yourselves servants to obey, his servants ye are to whom ye obey; whether of sin unto death, or of obedience unto righteousness?

I know that some of you, dear Readers, are still thinking, "I consider myself to be both saint and sinner." The above verse writes *finish* to that thinking; for sin always leads to spiritual death. We need to act in obedience to God to be judged righteous at our judgment.

Do you see how Paul is again referring to sin as a slave master? He is saying: Now that you have been set free from that master, see that you do not go back to him by yielding yourself to his orders. Hebrews 10:26–31 warns that committing one willful sin puts us back as a prisoner of sin. Sinning ends in a death for the sinner in the eternal lake of fire.

We have become free. We are freed to be willing and obedient slaves of our new master—Jesus, *our Lord and our God*. Go ahead and dance with joy! Don't worry about the Pharisees around you.

Faith without obedience avails nothing. The root meaning of the word *believe* includes "obedience." The translators of the King James Version of the Bible used the word *believe* to include obedience in Hebrews 3:18 and 4:6. The New King James Version has chosen the translation *obey* and *obedience* instead of *believe* and *unbelief*. Hebrews 3:13–14 says:

> But exhort [warn] one another daily, while it is called To day; lest any of you be hardened through the deceitfulness of sin. For we are made partakers of Christ, [only] if we hold the beginning of our confidence stedfast unto the end.

That is what this book is about. It is an exhortation to stay righteous and overcome sin and sinning. We obey God when we walk in the Spirit of Christ Jesus, as Romans 8:2 and 4 describe.

Romans 6:17

> But God be thanked, that ye were the servants of sin, but ye have obeyed from the heart that form of doctrine which was delivered you.

Paul emphasizes that we *were* the slaves of sin—not *are*. Once I had to obey sin. I thought that I had a choice, but I did not. I was a slave to sin! Slaves are not allowed to choose. Slaves obey.

We have heard it taught that God is slowly but surely aiming to set us free from sinning. Paul refutes that false teaching right here in verse 17.

Paul, Peter, John, and Jude all confirm the teaching of Jesus—that walking-in-Christ Christians are not sinners. Generally speaking, the church vehemently opposes their teaching that we are freed. By doing this, the church is unwittingly siding with Satan. As 1 John 3:8 says, anyone who sins is of the devil.

First John 1:6 states: "If we say that we have fellowship with [God], and walk in darkness [sin], we lie, and do not [know] the truth. We have already seen in previous verses that our eternal salvation stands or falls on the grace of Christ. His grace gives us a lifestyle of freedom from sin and sinning. Hebrews 12:15 warns us to be careful lest we fall short of that grace.

God keeps us faultless, according to Jude 24. But we must cooperate and obey Him and not let go of Him. Here is an example of Israel in the Old Testament:

> To whom did God swear that they would not enter His rest, but to those who did not obey Him.
>
> —Hebrews 3:18

> Since therefore it remains that some will enter that rest, remember that those to whom it was first preached failed to enter because of their disobedience
>
> —Hebrews 4:6

I can assure you this from personal experience. You cannot live freed from sin and sinning until you believe that you have been freed by your death with Christ and confess it from your heart and out of your mouth.

Jesus said, "Whosoever committeth sin is the servant of sin... If the Son therefore shall make you free, ye shall be free indeed" (John 8:34 and 36). Could anything be clearer than that? Paul says in Romans 6:11 that we have died to sin and have been made alive to God in Christ Jesus.

Peter gives the following warning:

> For if after they have escaped the pollutions of the world through the knowledge of the Lord and Saviour Jesus Christ, they are again entangled therein, and overcome, the latter end is worse with them than the beginning.
>
> —2 Peter 2:20

At one time, we were all sinners and had fallen short of the glory of God. But now, in Christ we are set free indeed:

> Whosoever abideth in him sinneth not: whosoever sinneth hath not seen him, neither known him.
>
> —1 John 3:6

Praise the Lord that the truth is once again being taught to us by the Holy Spirit! God's people in Jesus our Lord are beginning to shed the teaching of men. They are gladly accepting the Word of God; even though it means persecution and rejection from the "old wineskin brigade." Like Jesus, we will be made "perfect through sufferings" (Heb. 2:10).

Romans 6:18

> Being then made free from sin, ye became the servants [slaves] of righteousness.

This verse tells us who we are in Christ Jesus after we are born of water baptism and Spirit baptism.

RESTORING RIGHTEOUSNESS

> Jesus answered, Verily, verily, I say unto thee, Except a man be born of water and of the Spirit, he cannot enter into the kingdom of God.
>
> —JOHN 3:5

We have, in the words of Ephesians 4:24, become the new man of God, "created in [His] righteousness and true holiness" by His Spirit. We accept our new life in faith, and we also experience it. We no longer say "Jesus loves me, this I know, because the Bible tells me so." but "Jesus loves me this I know!" If we start to doubt God's promises of the new, sinless life, we will soon be taken captive by sin and revert to being the "old man." As Hebrews 10:38 teaches, the just must have a lifestyle of faith—not doubt.

Being a sinless person does not mean we are perfect. Being sinless is merely the start of the race set forth for us in Hebrews 12:1. We run by offering our body of flesh as a living sacrifice, according to the direction of Romans 12:1.

When we have the courage and trust to make this unconditional offering of our body—in sickness and in health, well fed or starving, young and strong or old and weak, accepting both the pain and the joy alike—we will discover "[God's] good, and acceptable, and perfect, will" for our lives (Rom. 12:1–2).

Do you desire to know the Lord's will for your life? Simply read and do what the previous paragraph says. Your faith, love, and "guts" will be sorely tested in the process, but there is no other way. Even Jesus had to do it. That's Bible!

The apostle Paul writes, "Examine yourselves as to whether you are in the faith. Test yourselves" (2 Cor. 13:5, NKJV).

> Hearken unto me, ye that know righteousness, the people in whose heart is my law; fear ye not the reproach of men, neither be ye afraid of their revilings.
>
> —ISAIAH 51:7

Chapter 14

RIGHTEOUSNESS AND HOLINESS!

ROMANS 6:19 SAYS:

> I speak after the manner of men because of the infirmity of your flesh: for as ye have yielded your members servants to uncleanness and to iniquity unto iniquity; even so now yield your members servants to righteousness unto holiness.

Holiness is having Godlike character. *Righteousness* is doing God's works. Paul uses the metaphor of a slave and a slave master because we all possess weak flesh.

He reminds us that, like all men, we were at one time sinners, slaves to sin. It is no use trying to deny that we were sinners for the apostle John states, "If we say that we have not sinned, we make [God] a liar, and his word is not in us" (1 John 1:10).

John gives us a similar warning in verse 8, "If we say that we have no sin, we deceive ourselves, and the truth is not in us." Again, he is referring to our sinful state before our conversion, not a sinful state after conversion.

In Romans 3:23 and 25, Paul says that all have, in the past, sinned and come short of the glory of God. Writing in 1 Timothy 1:13–15, he declares that he himself had been the greatest sinner.

There is no way out. We must face up to reality. Everyone is in the kingdom of darkness until Christ brings us into the kingdom of light, as 1 Peter 2:9 shows.

Paul teaches us what we need to do to secure our future, eternal salvation after we enter the kingdom of light. Without holiness, we will not see God. We will be condemned to outer darkness. The Hebrew word for *holiness* has the root meaning "to be blameless."

In verses 4–7 of his one-chapter letter, Jude states that anyone who teaches that God's grace covers Christian sinning is heading for condemnation. He implies that this doctrine denies our Lord Jesus Christ, for it denies that Christ will justly judge us on our deeds. It denies that Christ has set His people free from sin and sinning.

Can you imagine the elders of Israel telling the people in the desert of the Sinai Peninsula that they were not free from Pharaoh? It would have been laughable! Yet most of the church doctrines try to tell us that Christ has not set us completely free from sin.

Peter confirms Paul's teaching. He warns us about false teachers who teach that Christians who sin regularly are still acceptable to Him:

> For if God spared not the angels that sinned... And [these men likewise] shall receive the reward [for unrighteous

> behavior]...But it is happened unto them according to the true proverb, The dog is turned to his own vomit again.
>
> —2 Peter 2:4, 13, 22

He teaches in 1 Peter 2:24 that "we being dead to sins" are able to live righteously. We are healed from the disease of sin. Therefore, let us thank God through Jesus Christ that we have been healed of the disease of sin.

John writes: "Whosoever is born of God doth not commit sin; for his seed remaineth in him: and he cannot sin, because he is born of God" (1 John 3:9). Matthew 5:48 gives an order from God that Christians must be holy as our Father in heaven is holy. Holiness is not an option.

Romans 6:20

> For when ye were the servants of sin, ye were free from righteousness.

By now we should all be well aware that we were born under slavery to sin. Slaves cannot do their own will. Slaves must be obedient to their owner. By definition, a slave cannot have more than one owner. Therefore, we cannot be a slave to sin and a slave to righteousness at the same time. God intended us to be slaves to righteousness, but Adam sold us all to sin.

Paul uses the past tense to describe our condition before we came out of the kingdom of darkness into the kingdom of light in Jesus Christ. He says that we *were* slaves to sin.

But *now* our death with Christ has set us free from sin, our original master, and the Holy Spirit *now* rules us with the righteousness of Christ. It is all accomplished in us by our faith. We believe it and confess it and find ourselves walking in it.

Try to imagine yourself a slave to someone who flogged you and forced you to do horrible things every day. Finally, the time comes when you are on your deathbed, and all your family and friends are crying. Inwardly, however, you are rejoicing because death will release you forever from being a slave to wickedness.

Then, to your utter astonishment, as soon as you die you become resurrected and find yourself a slave who has been bought by the kindest, most merciful, and loving master on earth. Instead of having to do wickedness, you have to do only righteousness. Your new life delights you.

Dear Christian, you are that person! Accept your new life and walk in it by faith. The apostle John writes, "If ye know that he is righteous, ye know that every one that doeth righteousness is born of him" (1 John 2:29).

Jesus says in Matthew 7:26–27 that we must be *doers* of His words. It should be obvious that without continual obedience, no Christian will get the inheritance of seeing God for all eternity. Of course, it is possible to stumble without being disobedient. But it is a fine line.

Romans 6:21

> What fruit had ye then in those things whereof ye are now ashamed? for the end of those things [is] death.

Some of you may still have the mind-set that you only need to be a believer to have eternal life assured you at the end of the race. You have heard that your works do not count. But works do not count *only* for your initial redemption from the kingdom of darkness. Once we are in the kingdom of light, our eternal redemption depends wholly on our *doing* His works. First Peter 1:17 says, "the Father... without respect of persons judgeth according to every man's work."

Paul, in Romans 8:13, gives us a powerful reminder that if Christian believers revert to living after the flesh, they shall die. But *if through the Spirit* they "do mortify [kill off] the deeds of the body, [they] shall live."

Remembering that our new birth has made us like Adam, we can learn from him. Because he did not mortify the desire of his flesh and wanted more knowledge of God's law, he disobeyed God. He lost eternal life.

If he had continued to walk in obedience to God, he would have maintained eternal life. In the same way, I have to walk in obedience to the Spirit of God if I am to keep my eternal life. I received that life when, through my faith in Jesus Christ, God imputed righteousness to me. I became an "Adam-man" in Christ Jesus Himself, "the last Adam" described in 1 Corinthians 15:45.

Jesus, by His blood, reconciled us to God while we were still in our sins. Now it is up to us to stay clean by walking in obedience to Christ's Spirit, the Holy Spirit. Romans 5:9–10 says that we are "justified by [Christ's] blood" and "we shall be saved by his life."

God forbid that we should return to the lifestyle of which we are now ashamed. Matthew 12:33 and Romans 7:5 teach about the fruit of our lives. A bad tree presents bad fruit. Our fruit is our deeds. If our fruit is not good, our end is spiritual death. Rest assured that the world and the devil will again and again tempt you to doubt the death of your flesh and to return to being led by the flesh. Galatians 6:8 tells that he who is led by his flesh "shall of the flesh reap corruption." But he who is led by the Spirit "shall of the Spirit reap life everlasting."

For example, every time that I sit down to satisfy my hunger, the flesh desires that I go on eating until I become a glutton. On the other hand, when I am in obedience to the Spirit of Christ, I will be satisfied before I become bloated. The new man has to be led by the Spirit to avoid becoming, once again, a sinner. Worse still, Hebrews 10:26 and 12:15–17 warn that if the new man deliberately sins, there is no more sacrifice for sins available to him, even though he seeks it with tears.

The Spirit moderates the desires of our flesh, or, as the New King James Version of the Bible puts it, "the fruit of the Spirit is…self-control" (Gal. 5:22–23). It means that self seeks and accepts the control of the Spirit of God. This is the opposite of self alone being in control. Self-control without the Holy Spirit brings destruction. As Galatians 5:17 says, the desires of the flesh and the desire of the Spirit "are contrary the one to the other."

If you live in a city, I suggest that you take a weekend drive to an orchard. Ask the orchardist what he does with a tree that continues to bear bad fruit. Without hesitation his answer will be, "I cut it down and burn it." He burns it to get rid of any remains of its disease, so that the other trees will not be infected.

We must serve God acceptably in reverence and godly fear, for our God is a consuming fire, which He uses to destroy sinners. This is the solemn teaching of Hebrews 12:29, John 15:6, and Deuteronomy 4:24.

There is a hell of fire and there is an eternal lake of fire. Both are God's creation. I will leave you, dear Reader, to ponder these truths.

The Bible makes it abundantly clear that if Christians are to be true friends of God and man they must have a way of life that is careful to avoid sinning. They hate it in themselves and hate it in others. They will not justify it in themselves, and they will not justify it in others. They walk sinlessly by faith in Christ's promise that they are dead to sin and alive to God in Christ Jesus (Rom. 6:11).

> …my righteousness shall be for ever, and my salvation from generation to generation.
>
> —Isaiah 51:8

Chapter 15

Conditions Do Apply

Romans 6:22 says:

> But now being made free from sin, and become servants to God, ye have your fruit unto holiness, and the end everlasting life.

I voluntarily entered the waters of baptism in the name of Jesus Christ and experienced an immediate loss of interest in sinful attractions. Something happened! In baptism, I was evidencing my belief that in Christ my past sins had all been washed away. And, I was evidencing that I believe I died with Christ and that dead men are freed from sin. It was "faith-works," which bear witness to the unseen promises of God.

Hebrews 11:1 teaches that faith is "the evidence of things not seen." Faith is an action! Baptism is an opportunity to turn belief into faith.

I followed this baptism by asking for the baptism in the Holy Spirit. When Jesus decided to respond, I experienced a great and marvelous filling of His love. This love so overpowered me that from deep down inside of me, I immediately understood that I could now walk free from the attraction of sinful things for the rest of my life. But conditions apply—conditions such as obedience! I suggest that you give this book to anyone who is preparing for, or inquiring about, water baptism. It will ensure that they reap the benefits of their immersion. I believe that my water baptism and Spirit baptism fulfilled Jesus' instructions to Nicodemus—that a man needs to "be born of water and of the Spirit" before he can see and enter the kingdom of God (John 3:3, 5).

Since my Spirit baptism, I have always experienced His presence of love. It rises and falls as the tides of the ocean. Like the tidal flows, I have no say in the timing or intensity of His waves of love. Sometimes I will be resting on my couch, when suddenly a spasm of joy will shoot through my body. It seems to originate in my solar plexus at the pit of my stomach. I can think of nothing, as my mind goes blank. My body involuntarily jerks and flexes at the waist. I start groaning or simply hear myself repeating over and over, "O Jesus, O Jesus." I cannot focus my eyes on anything in the room, and I am completely intoxicated by my Lord's love. It can last for minutes or hours. I am at His disposal.

He says nothing. I say nothing, except the few words of His name which come from out of my belly and not from my brain. If I groan, it too originates from Him, somewhere within the region of my belly.

If I try to speak from my head to Him, the tide starts to recede. I can hear what is going on around me, but it seems to be at a distance.

But most of the time, the fruit of His presence, together with my faith that I am dead to sin and alive to God, keeps me doing righteously day by day. He gives me a holy lifestyle. I believe wholeheartedly with Paul that the end of holiness is everlasting life.

Saint Teresa of Avila wrote a warning in the sixteenth century that God's manifest presence may be lost, together with the soul, by willful sinning, ingratitude, or carelessly requiting His love.[1] Hebrews 10:26–31 expresses scriptural support for this statement.

Romans 6:23

> For the wages of sin is death; but the gift of God is eternal life through Jesus Christ our Lord.

First John 4:16 teaches that "God is love." Romans 5:5 tells us that the Holy Spirit pours God's love into our hearts. Therefore, we should not think it unusual to experience that God is present when, often for no apparent reason, the emotion of love sweeps through us. We experience His love within, and it can manifest outwardly through our body in various ways—often in laughter or tears. Love is an emotion, and I believe we should not be afraid of our emotions unless we stir them up for our self-gratification.

God motivates His people with faith, hope, and love, which come from Him. Any faith, hope, or love that originates from self is detrimental to the soul. Without Him, we can do nothing of any value in His sight. But the greatest of His three is love. For God is love! The Holy Spirit of grace brings God's love to our heart. In many ways, His comings and goings are more like a stream than the ocean tides. Every now and then, the heavy rains fall somewhere up in the distant mountain range, and suddenly the rivers quickly rise where no rain is seen. Sometimes, the rivers even overflow the banks that contain them. Just as suddenly, the waters subside, and the stream flows on again as usual.

In the Book of Kings, God speaks to His leader and says, "You shall not see wind nor rain, but this valley will be filled with water" (2 Kings 3:16–18). This is a picture of the Holy Spirit coming unannounced with the gift of Christ's love. No wonder He is called the Spirit of grace.

I have found that He may come daily, weekly, monthly, yearly. If He withdraws, it appears to be for the purpose of teaching me how to walk by faith without experience. I cannot please God without faith. These times may be called "dry times," and they are—in the sense that the stream is flowing normally, well below full.

Be aware that the fish in every stream wait longingly but patiently for the coming of the flood. For it is the raging torrent that allows them to travel far upstream to breed and bring forth a multitude of young. It is the Father's love that draws the sinner to His Son. Paul insists that nothing avails, "but *faith* which worketh by love" (Gal. 5:6).

My wife, my friends, my children, and I always attended church regularly, believed in Jesus as Lord and Savior, and prayed daily. However, it was not until we actively sought the baptism in the Holy Spirit and finally received Him that we started to experience His love *and* Him; our dearest Father who is love.

The worst teaching that ever came my way was that which said I had received the Holy Spirit as a believer and that there is no need to experience Him. In fact, it was generally understood that it was not good to expect to feel God's presence except inside a church or when I was reading the Bible. Like the Buddhists, I did not trust my emotions, even if they were to be activated by God. In fact, I was taught that any emotion I thought came from God would most likely be from the devil.

Dear Reader, if you want to continue being free from sin and sinning and have your fruit in holiness and eternal life, you must walk in the Holy Spirit. It is the Spirit Himself who gives life; the letter, according to 2 Corinthians 3:6, kills. Our faith in Jesus Christ for our eternal inheritance has to be a faith that believes His promises. If we do not believe that sinning prevents us from obtaining our inheritance of eternal salvation, our faith in Christ is a sham. Galatians 5:19–21 warns against the works of the flesh; God cannot be mocked, "for whatsoever a man soweth, that shall he also reap" (Gal. 6:7).

I have found that it is impossible for me to walk in the Spirit and experience God's love if I do not disassociate myself from the things of the world, which deaden my faith and the sense of His presence. For me, these things of the world are television (especially the news), drinking alcohol, smoking tobacco, reading newspapers or magazines, going to churches where the Holy Spirit is *not*, movies, parties, political discussions, taking medicines or prescribed drugs, and conversations which revolve around sports, sicknesses and health, or money and possessions. Please do not make what I do into a set of laws!

I have found that any of these things quench my own experience of God's presence, grieve the Spirit, and deaden my faith. I know that nothing the world offers can come anywhere near the satisfaction I receive from God's love and presence. For this reason, I shun the so-called pleasures and interests of the world. I tried them with full enthusiasm the first forty-eight years of my life, so I know what is best for me. I choose the delights of walking in the Spirit of Jesus Christ every time, and I encourage others to try it, for I find that they like it! I have been doing it for the past twenty-nine years, and it gets better all the time.

The Bible warns in James 4:4 that "whosoever…will be a friend of the world is the enemy of God." I agree. Don't you?

> In righteousness shalt thou be established: thou shalt be far from oppression; for thou shalt not fear: and from terror; for it shall not come near thee.
>
> —Isaiah 54:14

Chapter 16

Proud Humility?

We have come to the end of Romans 6. I am sure we do not need any special gifts to understand that it is simply a reminder from Paul that we have been freed from the stranglehold sin previously had on us.

But it is another matter to take it seriously and know that it is vital knowledge for us if we want to be saved at our judgment. Here we do need a revelation from the Holy Spirit.

This revelation, if accepted and confessed, will bring severe criticism and persecution from most brothers and sisters in the church. We will find ourselves in the company of our Savior.

Many church leaders will mock us and accuse us of pride, not realizing that it is a gross form of "prideful humility" for a Christian to confess that he will be a sinner till he dies. If we believe that Romans, chapters 6–8, is the nuts and bolts of the righteous lifestyle we need for eternal salvation, it will certainly make you unacceptable with most churches. We will find ourselves isolated and on a very narrow road. Take heart, for Jesus says in Matthew 7:14 that few are on the narrow road. Have no fears, He will sustain you.

Christ's one purpose in coming to earth as a man was to take away the sin of the world. John 1:29 records the witness of John the Baptist, "Behold the Lamb of God, which taketh away the sin of the world." And, as 1 John 3:8 says, "For this purpose the Son of God was manifested, that he might destroy the works of the devil."

These scriptures are not talking about forgiveness of sins, but the end of sinning. Jesus Christ has written *finish* to the law of sin, as Romans 8:2 teaches. I believe He did it and I accept it. It works! I walk freed from sinning, according to Romans 8:4 and 1 John 3:6.

Charles Finney taught, "Christians think they are to remain in sin, and all they hope for is forgiveness and holiness in heaven! But the whole framework of the Gospel is designed to break the power of sin and fill men with all the fullness of life. If the Church would read the Bible and lay hold of every promise, they would find them great and precious."[1]

> No weapon that is formed against thee shall prosper; and every tongue that shall rise against thee in judgment thou shalt condemn. This is the heritage of the servants of the Lord, and their righteousness is of me, saith the Lord.
>
> —Isaiah 54:17

Chapter 17

What about 1 John 1:8–10?

If you, dear Reader, are acquainted with the church teachings of the New Testament, you may well be thinking that Paul's Romans 6 conflicts with 1 John 1:8–10. These scriptures in John's first letter are persistently misused by Christian sinners wrongfully to justify that their sinning is a normal condition for all who follow Christ.

Are they right? It has been said that a drowning man will even clutch at a sharp razor in an effort to stay afloat. But if Paul is teaching one thing and John another, then the Bible cannot be accepted as truth.

However, the Bible is the truth, and the two apostles are not contradicting each other, as I will now explain as plainly as I can.

When we look for an author's intended meaning in any written words, we need to seek confirmation in two or three other places in their writings. In New Testament writings, we must also seek confirmation from the other writers of the epistles and from Jesus' teachings in the Gospels.

Using the biblical principle of needing two or three witnesses to confirm a truth, we will begin with 1 John 1:8. It declares:

> If we say that we have no sin, we deceive ourselves, and the truth is not in us.

This verse agrees with Paul's teachings on sinning as found in Romans 6, if it is taken to mean the sins committed *before* we are born of God. What John is saying is this: we are deceiving ourselves if, after being born of God through faith in Jesus Christ, we say or think that we did not sin before our conversion.

Confirmation that John is indeed referring to our sinning *before* rebirth comes from the following scriptures:

> Jesus answered them, Verily, verily, I say unto you, Whosoever committeth sin is the servant of sin... If the Son therefore shall make you free, ye shall be free indeed.
>
> —JOHN 8:34, 36

And, John himself teaches, just two verses before the controversial verse 8:

> If we say that we have fellowship with him, and walk in darkness [sin], we lie, and do not the truth.
>
> —1 JOHN 1:6

Therefore, if verse 8 is mistakenly thought to mean that Christians deceive themselves if they say that they are not continuing to be sinners after conversion, it means that John is a fool who is flatly contradicting his statement two verses beforehand. For there he states that any Christian who continues sinning (in darkness) and thinks to himself that he is still okay with God makes himself a liar.

John is not a fool. Verse 8 can logically agree with verse 6 only if we understand that verse 8 is talking about sins we committed *before* we were born of God.

Further on in the same letter, John confirms the real meaning of verse 8 over and over:

> Whosoever abideth in him sinneth *not*: whosoever sinneth hath not seen him, neither known him.
>
> —1 JOHN 3:6

And:

> If a man abide not in me, he is cast forth as a branch, and is withered; and men gather them, and cast them into the fire, and they are burned.
>
> —JOHN 15:6

And:

> Anyone who commits sin is of the devil [Satan], for the devil sinneth from the beginning. For this reason the Son of God was manifested so that the workings of the devil [sinning] could be destroyed.
>
> —1 JOHN 3:8, *NESTLES GREEK TEXT*

And:

> Whosoever is born of God doth not commit sin; for his seed remaineth in him: and he cannot sin, because he is born of God.
>
> —1 JOHN 3:9

With those six separate confirmations, we can undeniably confirm that John does not teach that Christians are sinners after their conversion. Only fools make a statement and then proceed to contradict themselves! I do not think that anyone could consider John to be a fool. After all, he was one of the most prolific writers in the New Testament.

No, it is clear that in verse 8 our beloved John is reminding us to not have the foolish impression that we were not sinners *before* we were born of the Spirit. He continues in verse 9 and says, "Confess those pre-conversion sins (the sinner's prayer), and you will be cleansed." He implies that we should not stubbornly go on and say or think that we were not sinners.

In complete denial of Christ's promise and the teachings of Paul and Peter and John's epistle, most of the church persists in teaching that John is saying: "Do not say you are not sinning. But confess your continued sinning, and you will be cleansed."

I ask myself why so many in the church are denying that we are set free from sin and sinning in Christ. The reason, I believe, is that they are teaching on what they themselves see and feel and not on faith in the Word of God. I have found that Christians who are bound by sinning base their whole walk on a complete misunderstanding of 1 John 1:8–10. It is their great comfort, and it is of the devil. They believe the same lie he told Eve in Genesis 3:4. "Ye shall not surely die [if you disobey God]." In the end, they will be destroyed!

In his second letter, Peter tells us that if we forget that we were purged from our *old* sins, we are like a blind person who "cannot see afar off" (2 Pet. 1:9). John goes on to say in 1 John 2:1 that his purpose in writing his letter is so that we do not sin. Of course John and Paul both realized that it is possible for a Christian to temporarily lose faith and so stumble unwillingly into sinning. John uses the significant word *if* to show that it would be the exception and not the rule.

> My little children, these things write I unto you, that ye sin not. And if any man sin, we have an advocate with

> the Father, Jesus Christ the righteous.
>
> —1 JOHN 2:1

John then looks Christians straight in the eye and says:

> He that saith, I know [God], and keepeth not his commandments [sins], is a liar, and the truth [Jesus] is not in him.
>
> —1 JOHN 2:4

This is the same John writing in the same letter that most of the church claims teaches the opposite—that we are living sinful lives and make sure we confess it. Otherwise we will be making God to be a liar.

However, the truth is that to avoid being liars, as described in 1 John 1:6 and 2:4, we must accept the evidence that 1 John 1:8–10 is talking about our way of life leading up to our conversion to Christ. It is not about our condition after we have been forgiven and reconciled to God.

It is pridefully humble to confess, "I am a sinner." I know. I did it for years before I saw the truth.

But true humility is to declare that we are not sinning because we know full well that it is only the grace of our Lord and nothing of our own striving that keeps us that way. It is only by our faith in Him and His promises that we are leading a righteous lifestyle!

When it is no longer I who live but Christ, how can I be arrogant as the devil would desire? (Gal. 2:20.) I cannot!

It is observable that many Christians do not experience true conversion and freedom because they have failed to have the revelation that they were previously sinners headed for destruction. This is why John wrote verses 8–10 in his letter to Christians. He is telling them to wake up and confess that they sinned in the past.

Christ shed His lifeblood so that we, according to Romans

5:10, can be saved from being sinners and go on to eternal salvation by His life in us. Hebrews 12:14 says that without holiness, no man will see God. Christ imparts His holiness to us, and our lifestyle is holy in Him as we walk in His Spirit.

If we put our own past experiences ahead of God's Word, we can find it very consoling to accept the wrong interpretation of 1 John 1:8–10. However, by reading the next two chapters of his letter together with Romans, chapters 6–8, it will be seen that all Christians need to say the sinner's prayer at their conversion and walk sinlessly in Him after baptism.

If Christ cannot set me free from sinning, I am not much better than a Jew of the Old Testament. For a Jew could also have sins he "committed in ignorance" forgiven by the offering of blood (Heb. 9:7, NKJV).

Personally, I do not need a Christ who cannot set me free from sinning. But praise the Lord, He *has* set me free from sinning, and I intend to tell everyone and spread the word of truth. Jesus Christ redeemed me at great cost—His life! He did it so that He could possess me, and He does.

I do not have to avoid preaching scriptures that appear to be contradictory, for I find no disagreement. I do not blindly follow another person's interpretations of Scripture or my own thoughts and experience. I go to the New Testament, which is the Word of God, and work on it until the Holy Spirit brings agreement by the confirmation of two or three witnesses. I warn every Christian that Romans 6 is at the very heart of their eternal salvation at their judgment.

If Christians doubt God's promise that Christ has set them free from sin and sinning, it will not be long before they fall back into the hands of Satan. But are we warned that anyone who sins is of the devil?

In 2 Peter 3:16, Peter said that Paul's writings had "some things hard to be understood, which they that are unlearned and unstable wrest, as they do also the other scriptures, unto their own destruction."

Peter, Paul, John, Jude, and our Lord Jesus all taught that born-again, Spirit-led Christians cannot sin. John Wesley, Hudson Taylor, Watchman Nee, Charles Spurgeon, Charles Finney, and William Seymour (the first Pentecostal preacher at the Azusa Street chapel) all believed it, too.

First John 3:10 says:

> In this the children of God are manifest, and the children of the devil: whosoever doeth not righteousness [is a sinner and] is not of God, neither he that loveth not his brother [in the Lord].

But you might be thinking that John's first letter says we are all sinners. Dear Christian, I leave it to you to decide. As for me and my brothers and sisters, we believe that 1 John teaches that everyone is a sinner before conversion. After conversion, we do not sin if we abide in Jesus Christ and are born of God. All the New Testament writers agree with us.

Your decision could determine where you spend eternity!

My prayer is this:

> *That we will allow you, Lord, to unstop our ears and open our blind eyes in these times of trouble, to see and hear what the epistles really say about sin and sinning. Teach us to accept that You are the victorious overcomer of sin, that in You we have the victory. Remind and show us again of the seventy-four New Testament chapters that warn us against sinning. Do not let us forget that a Christian who sins is more responsible and accountable before you than a sinner in the world. Keep us aware that the judgment starts with us, that any deliberate sinning can quickly become unforgivable, and that all sinning crucifies the Son of God afresh. We can see that every church split and denomination starts from pride and stubbornness on both sides. We do not make time to patiently sit down together and listen to the Holy Spirit until we reach His way for unity and*

> *agreement. I believe that it is never too late to start afresh and that you are waiting. Dear God, help us! Amen.*

Paul's next chapter (seven) is another stunner from God's throne room. Be prepared to have your faith tested. You will be asked to discard a cherished wineskin.

Romans 7 gives a detailed description of the frustrating life of a person under the Law, a life that is not led by the Spirit. The apostle Paul starts by reminding Christians that their faith-death with Christ also has separated them from the written Law that was given to Moses. He is warning the freed, baptized believer of chapter 6 not to return to a life under the written Law. He says that living under the written Law keeps a person under another law, the law of sin. This is the first time in the entire Bible that we find the term *the law of sin*. It is a law that says sin always forces natural mankind to commit sins, even though it is against a person's fully determined willpower to obey God's law.

> Blessed are they which do hunger and thirst after righteousness: for they shall be filled.
>
> —Matthew 5:6

Chapter 18

Two Tigers

We are now about to enter an arena where two opposing tigers are pacing up and down, glaring at each other in a false peace. It is a conflict over the meaning of Romans 7. There can be only one truth, so let us search it out in love. We either have the truth, or we have a lie!

The larger of the tigers represents Christians who believe they will go on sinning until they depart from earthly life. Therefore, with that false premise they interpret this chapter 7 as a description of the typical life of a "normal," sinning Christian. But they are also prepared to tolerate the opposing view that maybe, just maybe, there is another interpretation. Perhaps they believe that peace is better than truth. But Buddha also teaches peace at any price. Perhaps they forget that Paul did not break his original letter into chapters, and therefore the last few questions posed in Romans 7 cannot be separated from the answer given in chapter 8.

The tiger that is considerably smaller represents Christians who believe that Romans 7 is a description of mankind before (and not after) conversion. They do not prefer peace to truth. They treat chapters 6-8 as a whole and do not divide them up piecemeal. Their premise is in agreement with Romans 8:2, which declares that we who are in Christ Jesus have been freed from the law of sin and sinning. It is in agreement with the declaration of their King—Jesus—who says that he whom the Son sets free from sinning is "free indeed" (John 8:36).

Their belief is founded on Scripture, while the Christians of the big tiger base their beliefs on sight—present and past experience. I challenged a pastor/author of a large evangelical church in Chicago about why he stood on the side of the big tiger. His reply did not contain one shred of scriptural backing, but he said, "If I accept your teaching, I will be out of a job. Most of my life is taken up with counseling the sinners in our church." His words epitomize the big-tiger philosophy that walks in this arena by sight and not by faith in the promises of Scripture.

The big tiger always turns out to be a paper tiger. Personally, I make no excuses, but openly declare the truth in love. I reach for the stars! Our sister, Teresa of Avila, claims that Jesus appeared to her many times and once said:

> All the harm that befalls the world comes from the failure to understand the truths of Scripture in all their clarity.[1]

Considering the fact that up to five hundred different Christian denominations have spawned from Scripture, it appears that Teresa heard Him correctly.

I believe that Romans 7 is the most misunderstood chapter in all the New Testament letters. A wrong understanding of this letter assists the devil in keeping Christians beset by sins. But, as Romans 6:23 says, "The wages of sin is death."

Keep in mind that Paul spoke about eternal life earlier in his letter:

> [God] will render to every man according to his deeds [works]: To them who by patient continuance in well doing seek for glory and honour and immortality, eternal life.
>
> —Romans 2:6–7

It is therefore obvious that Paul's whole teaching on how to obtain our Christian inheritance of eternal life is dependent on what we do and not just on who we are. And Paul got it from Jesus our Lord.

Charles Finney sees it clearly: "Most Christians see Christ as Saviour, the propitiation of their sins, to make atonement and procure forgiveness—and then they stop. After that it is often exceedingly difficult to get their attention that Christ is their Savior from further sinning. They feel that they don't need Him for this purpose!"[2]

> Blessed are they which are persecuted for righteousness' sake: for theirs is the kingdom of heaven.
>
> —Matthew 5:10

Chapter 19

LAW IS NOT IN THE GRAVE!

ROMANS 7:1 SAYS:

> Know ye not, brethren [the "Christian Jews"], (for I speak to them that know the law,) how that the law hath dominion over a man as long as he liveth?

As you will remember, Paul has previously hinted at the danger of being under the Law. In Romans 6:14 he stated that "sin shall not have dominion [control]" over any Christian who *is not* under the Law. Now, in chapter 7, he goes into the nuts and bolts of the connection between sin and the Law. In this first verse he wants anyone who has been instructed in the Law to realize that laws apply only to a person whose body is still breathing.

Romans 7:2

> For the woman which hath an husband is bound by the law to her husband so long as he liveth; but if the husband be dead, she is loosed [released] from the law of her husband.

Paul knows that for some of us it is not obvious that laws are only applicable to the living. Therefore he gives an illustration of the law of marriage and the way death nullifies that law. He reinforces how important it is for a Christian to be acutely aware of his faith-death with Christ's death.

It is hard to be eternally saved at the Judgment Day unless we know every day and every moment that our old man is dead on Christ's cross. Death brings freedom from sin and also freedom from the impossible task of trying to use the Law of written commandments to keep us from doing wrong. Galatians 2:21 says, "If righteousness [could] come by the law, then Christ is dead in vain." He wasted His time in dying for us.

Romans 6 speaks about being freed by death from the power of sin. Romans 7 is about being freed by death from the Law of commandments, which, according to 1 Corinthians 15:56, gives sin its power.

We will learn from the following scriptures that we cannot be righteous Christians by trying to obey the written Law of right and wrong, which Moses received from God at Mount Sinai. Whether it shocks me or not, this is a New Testament truth on which the life of grace and redemption stands or falls. As Romans 10:4 says, "Christ is the end of the law for righteousness to every one that believeth."

Romans 7:3

> So then if, while her husband liveth, she be married to another man, she shall be called an adulteress: but if her

> husband be dead, she is free from that law; so that she is no adulteress, though she be married to another man.

Here Paul continues to show that because of death, the sixth of the Ten Commandments obviously no longer applies. He is using this repetitive verse to make a second witness to his teaching that dead persons are freed from the Law and ready for a new marriagelike covenant with Christ.

Romans 7:4

> Wherefore, my brethren [in Christ], ye also are become dead to the law by the body of Christ; that ye should be married to another, even to him who is raised from the dead [Jesus Christ], that we should bring forth fruit unto God.

Paul now goes on and draws the comparison that the Jews were in a sense married to the Law. Now, since they have died with Christ, they are freed—like a widow—from the whole set of written laws that had bound them before they died.

When Christ's body of flesh died, my carnal body died too. It becomes a reality for me by faith in the above scripture. Therefore I am released from the written Law of the Ten Commandments. I am so happy because they, as we noted before, are what gives power to sin.

I know I cannot enter into eternal life at the judgment if I have lived under the written Law. If this offends you, please do not throw this book away, for I am quoting the Bible.

We had to die so that we could be free, like a lady whose husband has died, to be joined to another—Jesus Christ, the living law of God. Our new marriage will conceive and birth good spiritual fruit, such as love, joy, and peace. Ephesians 5:9 says, "For the fruit of the Spirit is in all goodness and righteousness and truth." We have come under the Law of the Spirit of life in Christ Jesus. The written Law on the other hand brought death, as 2 Corinthians 3:6 shows.

I cannot serve two masters. Christ, at my baptism *into His name*, took me to death. Why? To free me from sin, my old master, and its driving force, which is the Ten Commandments that were written on stone tablets. Now I have a new master, the resurrected Christ Jesus! He lives forever. He lives in me!

My dear reader, if you call yourself a Christian and yet continue using the Ten Commandments for your knowledge of what is right and wrong, you are on the same road as Adam and his wife, Eve. They thought that they knew better than God and disobeyed Him by imbibing in the fruit of the "law tree" of the knowledge of good and evil. Sadly, they tried to mix law knowledge with trust in God alone. We need to learn a lesson from their bad example, which brought them spiritual death. Trust God alone by His Spirit. Be led of the Spirit. Otherwise at the end of the road you will be a castaway.

Romans 7:5

> For when we were in the flesh, the motions of sins, which were by the law, did work in our members to bring forth fruit unto death.

Fruit unto spiritual death is any sinful word or deed that the Bible calls unrighteous works. God's ultimate punishment for sins is the second death in the everlasting lake of fire.

In the flesh means that we live under the desires of our body. Earlier in this letter, Paul warned us that our natural, fleshly desires are controlled by a force called sin, which unfailingly turns our desires into uncontrollable lust and sinning. The official Bible definition of *sinning*, found in 1 John 3:4, is transgressing (breaking) any of the written Law of God.

Paul in Galatians 5:14 reminds us that "all the law is fulfilled in one word, even in this; Thou shalt love thy neighbour as thyself." Therefore, we sin when we insult or disobey God; or in any way unjustly hurt another person. It includes disobeying authority; unless that authority directs us to knowingly commit a sin.

The Ten Commandments pinpoint the blatantly obvious sins but cannot help us stop sinning. In fact they empower sinning, as 1 Corinthians 15:56 teaches.

If the Law could set us free from sinning, there would have been no need for Christ to come down from heaven to earth to be crucified. The New Testament says that Christ is the end of the Law for obtaining righteousness. Under the Law, "There is none righteous, no, not one" (Rom. 3:10). We are sinners and "come short of the glory [requirements] of God" (Rom. 3:23). The Law, according to Galatians 2:21, frustrates God's grace.

Any religion that teaches we can become righteous by trying to obey the Ten Commandments or any set of supporting laws will, on the contrary, produce sinners instead of saints. For example, eating a meat pie on a Friday is only unlawful for a person under a law that forbids it. Not paying a tithe to a church is only sinful to the one who is under a law of tithing. Further into the chapter we will find Paul's teaching that mankind was unaware that coveting is evil until the written Law of the Ten Commandments declared it so.

The written Law of God, because of the weakness of the flesh of mankind, actually produces the worst type of sinners. From it come hypocrites, who, in Jesus' day, were generally the scribes and Pharisees of the state religion, under bondage to the Law.

The teachings of the new covenant took effect when the Holy Spirit came at the feast of Pentecost, fifty days after the Crucifixion of our Lord Jesus. These teachings unquestionably declare that laws, especially the Ten Commandments, produce sinners. They are described as a dividing wall between Jew and non–Jew, a wall that Christ, by His death, "abolished in His flesh" (Eph. 2:14–16).

Christ Himself became for us the living law of God. He

is our law! He fulfilled it. He did away with the written laws and incorporated them all in one unwritten law of love, as described in Galatians 5:13–14. In Romans 8:2, Paul calls it the law of the Spirit of Life in Christ Jesus.

It is a deceit from Satan that has crept into church doctrines allowing Christians to suppose that since Christ's atonement covers their past sins that they can presume continuing forgiveness. But they are thereby heading toward the unforgiveable sin and mocking God (Heb. 10:26–31; Gal. 6:7). They don't see that the gospel demands and has made provision to rid us forever from all sin. They look at it as a system of pardon, leaving the sinner to drag His load to the gates of heaven (and be refused admittance), for without holiness no man will be allowed to see God (Heb. 12:14).

> Let your light so shine before men, that they may see your good works, and glorify your Father which is in heaven.
>
> —Matthew 5:16

Chapter 20

Our Deliverance From the Law

Romans 7:6 says:

> But now we are delivered from the law, that being dead wherein we were held; that we should serve in newness of spirit, and not in the oldness of the letter [the written Law].

Take great heed, all Christians who think you can continue under the Ten Commandments. Galatians 5:4 warns:

> Christ is become of no effect unto you, whosoever of you are justified by the law; ye are fallen from grace.

Romans 7:6 reveals that all who are under the law become

spiritually dead. Therefore, Christ came to "to redeem them that were under the law" (Gal. 4:5).

I am under the living Spirit of God. It is a new life! He is my conscience.

What sort of a father would present his wife and children with a set of written laws, a list of commands and duties to be carried out every day? Do you not know that Jesus had a deliverance ministry? He came to deliver you and me from sin and the written law of commandments, which empower sin.

Have you accepted your deliverance from these two controllers? Please stop and think about this before you shrug it off with an *of course*. Jesus delivered us by taking us to death with Him! Dead mankind cannot commit sin, and dead mankind is not under the Law.

You have just read the good news of the gospel of Christ! In our new life, we are under the law of Jesus Christ. We have grown up under the doctrine that Christians can expect to go on sinning until death-do-us-part. But we have learned from Romans 6 that we are already dead and freed from sin.

In Romans 5:8, Paul wrote, "But God commendeth his love toward us, in that, while we were yet sinners, Christ died for us." He does not say while we *are* yet sinners, but he uses the past tense *were* sinners. We have too easily accepted the poisonous brainwashing of man, that we are still sinners. Without question, it is now time to let the pure water of the Word of faith and truth wash that poison, which is taking us to eternal death, from our brains.

Therefore, I invite you to join me and, by faith, "put on the new man, which after God is created in righteousness and true holiness" (Eph. 4:24). I consider it stupidity to go back to the Ten Commandments or church laws to find righteousness. They have proved to be unable to keep mankind from falling into sin. But if I trust in Jesus for righteousness, He has promised that He is able to keep us from falling back into sin and "present [us] faultless before the presence of his glory with exceeding joy" (Jude 24).

Romans 7:7

> What shall we say then? is the law sin? God forbid [of course not]. Nay, I had not known sin, but by the law: for I had not known lust [illegal desire], except the law had said, Thou shalt not covet [the ninth and tenth commandments].

This verse shows us that this chapter 7 is about the Ten Commandments that were written on tablets of stone and were the basis of God's Law, His covenant with His people. I have spoken to the elders of many of the Pacific Islands, and they all tell me that coveting was never wrong for them until the missionaries brought them the Ten Commandments.

It seems that when we cannot bring the Spirit, we turn back to preaching the written Law. The Law may change us from being savages to civilized, but it does not change the evil heart of mankind.

The commandments themselves cannot be sinful because they come from God. The knowledge of what is good and evil is not sinful, and God never said it is. So what is wrong with the Law? That's a good question, and the answer is coming soon!

Romans 7:8

> But sin, taking occasion by the commandment, wrought in me all manner of concupiscence [sinful lust]. For without the law sin was dead.

God said to Adam:

> Of every tree of the garden thou mayest freely eat: But of the tree of the knowledge of good and evil, thou shalt not eat of it: for in the day that thou eatest thereof thou shalt surely die.
>
> —Genesis 2:16–17

God was talking about spiritual death, which separates man from Him. He was telling Adam that obtaining His laws of good and evil would result in the entrance of sin into his life. Sin controls us and keeps us sinning. Romans 6:23 reminds us that "the wages of sin is death." Disobedient Adam and his wife both experienced spiritual death as a result of eating the fruit of the tree of the knowledge of good and evil, and later physical death.

Sin in man uses the commandments to work all types of uncontrollable evil desires in him. Where there is no law, sin is as good as dead.

Are you teaching your son or daughter that the Ten Commandments will keep them righteous? Are you teaching this to new converts? If so, you are putting people who have been converted back under sin—and death. Your children and your converts may change for the better on the surface, but inside they are worse than before. Only their faith in the Spirit of life in Jesus Christ can keep them from falling.

Children and converts alike need a change of heart. They need the impartation of the Spirit of truth. The Spirit of God changes an evil heart to a good heart; but He must be allowed to work apart from and not with the written Law of commandments. We cannot mix the Law and the Spirit without producing the worst type of evil. God shut Adam and Eve out of the Garden of Eden so that they would not be able to also eat of the tree of life. The tree of life being the Spirit of Jesus Christ. He was protecting them from thinking that they had become as God.

The written Law is like an old wineskin. If new wine is put in it, we lose both the new wine and the old wineskin. Jesus is the new wine. He alone is "the way, the truth, and the life" (John 14:6).

Romans 7:9

> For I was alive without the law once: but when the commandment came, sin revived, and I died.

Remember that Paul, for the sake of making chapter 7 vivid to the reader, uses the pronoun *I* to stand for mankind. In the above verse he points out that Adam and Eve were spiritually alive and without the Law at the beginning of mankind. They did not know good from evil. But after they ate the fruit of the knowledge of good and evil in disobedience, God's law entered their minds. Genesis 3:1–10 tells how they thereby acquired a conscience and therefore justly suffered spiritual death. Conscience is the result of the law of God written in the hearts of all Adam's descendants.

Paul wrote Romans 7 to teach mankind that the Law is spiritually fatal to any person who touches it. When we read the word *I* in this epistle, we can put our own name in it, and often it will help us get the real meaning of this message of God-given truth.

Adam and Eve showed that we, in our human, fleshly nature, are intrigued by the Law of God. But as Paul says in the above verse, the Law brings spiritual death. God had warned Adam, but man seems to have to learn the hard way!

Later on, in Romans 8:14, Paul teaches that we must be led by the Spirit to be sons and daughters of God. We need a living Holy Spirit conscience.

Physical death sets us free from the Law. Christ took me to death with Him. Therefore Paul warns me not to revive sin's power again by looking to the Law. The Law is good, but sin uses it to kill me.

Romans 7:10

> And the commandment, which was ordained to life, I found to be unto death.

Adam and Moses and the followers of Moses discovered and continue, to this day, to discover that we cannot obtain a righteous life (sinless living) by the Law of the Ten Commandments. Paul writes the remainder of Romans 7 to explain why we need an alternative to the commandments if we are to possess a sinless lifestyle and thereby avoid the spiritual death that comes from sinning. He will reveal that our original, imputed righteousness has to become a righteous lifestyle of holiness if we are to see God. He will tell us how to do it.

First John 3:9 states that we cannot commit sin if we are born of God. Paul, on the other hand, never speaks in any of his letters about being "born of God." Instead, he uses the term *walking in the Spirit* and says that only those who are being led by the Spirit of God, according to Romans 8:14, are His sons (*sons* means "born of God").

Therefore, we can learn from Paul that being born of God is a day-by-day walk of faith. It is achievable because, as 1 John 3:9 says, God's seed, the Spirit of Jesus Christ, remains in us. If I am to walk in holiness, it is critical for me to be aware that being born of God is a state of walking by faith in the Spirit day by day. Please study the verses I have referenced until you can understand that what I am saying is scripturally correct.

Anyone who is in sin can no longer claim to be born again. That is the reason that Jesus told Nicodemus in John 3:5 that a man must be born of God (born of the Spirit to enter the kingdom of God.

Romans 7:11

> For sin, taking occasion by the commandment, deceived me, and by it slew me.

Sin is the great deceiver that lives in the body of flesh of every human. In the time between Adam and the Law given to Moses, everyone had the law written in their hearts, and their conscience showed this. Romans 2:12 says:

> For as many as have sinned without law shall also perish without law: and as many as have sinned in the law shall be judged by the law.

But, as Romans 7:13 says, "sin by the commandment [becomes] exceeding sinful." Therefore, God sent His Son to "redeem them that were under the law" (Gal. 4:5).

The Law gives power to sin and sinning brings spiritual death. However, you may say with Paul that the Law was given for life. Yes, but Paul also reminds us that it always turns out to bring us death. Carnal mankind cannot consistently obey laws. It's a fact of life.

But sin cannot rule the Spirit-led man. Sin rules the flesh-man because the flesh is weak and under sin. It runs riot when the Spirit-led man holds on to the Law of commandments. Such a man is neither hot nor cold, but lukewarm, the worst possible case, according to Revelation 3:15.

Romans 7:12

> Wherefore the law is holy, and the commandment holy, and just, and good.

Look at it this way. A racing car is a good thing, and so is an airplane. So are little children. But if we allow a little child to take the controls of these machines, it spells disaster.

Likewise the Law is good and the Ten Commandments, but when man tries to use them—disaster. The fault is in the user! Mankind is born carnal, and carnal man cannot live in any sort of harmony without some form of laws of right and wrong.

But God demands the opposite. He says that His spiritual men must not follow even one written law, for the Spirit-led man must live by a living law. It is called the law of the Spirit of life in Christ Jesus. He is the living Word of God, who "is quick, and powerful, and sharper than any two-edged sword...and is a discerner of the thoughts and intents of the heart" (Heb. 4:13). The law of the Spirit cannot, and must not, be written. We will look at it in Roman 8. The written Law kills, but the Spirit brings life, as 2 Corinthians 3:6 testifies.

ROMANS 7:13

> Was then that which is good made death unto me? God forbid. But sin, that it might appear sin, working death in me by that which is good; that sin by the commandment might become exceeding sinful.

At first, God used the simple, straightforward approach. He said to mankind, "Do not eat of the knowledge of my laws of good and evil" (Gen. 2:17). We disobeyed!

God's second try was along the lines of what we know as learning-the-hard-way, by experience. Most parents are driven to the same teaching pattern for their sons and daughters. When our children do not heed our advice, we put them out into the real world, where they will learn for themselves. But it is painful to both parent and child.

When God decided to give Moses a set of written laws of good and evil, He was putting His children on a learning curve they would be on for more than fifteen hundred years. They were to learn from painful experience that the more laws we have and the more that we strive to keep them, the more we break them.

We should understand by now that we are forced to commit sins by a power that comes from the knowledge of written laws. Three thousand five hundred years later, most of us have not learned it.

Jesus came and took us to death to the Law but few believe it. God required Adam, Abraham, and His Son, Jesus, to walk solely by faith in Him and not in the knowledge of His laws. He tells us to do the same in Galatians 4:21–30.

Walking by faith in Jesus Christ and His promises is the only way to be holy and blameless in our lifestyle and thereby gain entry into the eternal kingdom of Jesus Christ. Acts 4:12 clearly states that "there is none other name...whereby we must be saved" from the lake of fire on Judgment Day. We make it home by trusting only in the name of His Son.

Therefore relying on help from anyone but Jesus and His Spirit—or from any laws—bars us from our inheritance in heaven. Jesus will be our judge on that day, and our judge is not swayed by anyone, no matter what so-called influence or assurance they may think they possess. First Peter 1:17 explains that He judges me on my works (my lifestyle) and is no respecter of persons, even those who cry, "Lord, Lord!" (Matt. 7:21–27).

Romans 7:14

> For we know that the law is spiritual: but I am carnal, sold under sin.

From this verse, we know for certain that Paul is writing about mankind—including himself—before conversion to Christ by the Spirit. Before conversion, we were all sold under sin. But at conversion, we have accepted that He has bought us back from sin and reconciled us to our Father. John 8:34 and 36 describes the change Christ made by redeeming us from the grasp of sin and death. As we continue to abide in Him, according to 1 John 3:6, we do not sin. Romans 6:17–18 shows how Paul and you and I were once the slaves of sin, but now we are slaves of righteousness.

All mankind is born carnal. The word *carnal* means "flesh." All flesh has been sold by our first parents to a slave master called sin. In Romans 7:14, Paul is not talking about Spirit-led persons. He is telling flesh-led people, who try to follow written moral laws, not to do it.

I will repeat: Paul wrote chapter 7 to teach people who are under the Law of commandments that while they remain that way, they cannot be set free from sinning and its punishment, death.

He calls it another law—the law of sin. It forces all who are under the Law of commandments to be sinners, even against their will. We will learn more about the law of sin in verses 21–23.

Galatians 2:11–16 tells how Paul had found that he needed to teach the apostle Peter the same lesson about being under the Law. In the context of this, he said:

> ...if, while we seek to be justified by Christ, we ourselves also are found sinners, is therefore Christ the minister of sin? God forbid. For if I build again the things which I destroyed, I make myself a transgressor. For I through the law am dead to the law, that I might live unto God.
>
> —GALATIANS 2:17–19

In those verses, Paul is warning Christians that if they return to the Law of commandments, they will again become transgressors (sinners). But horror of horrors, if we are found to be sinners, we leave Christ open to the charge that He produces sinners. I hope the present-day church will realize this when it comes to an understanding of these three verses. If we claim that Christians are *still* sinners but saved by grace, we are insulting the Spirit of Jesus Christ and are an abominable state of affairs in the sight of God. It brings disgrace on the name of Jesus Christ and His people. For this reason Paul wrote the Corinthian church leaders and, in 1 Corinthians 5:13, told them to toss out blatant sinners.

The Law of commandments was given to teach carnal mankind that by it they could never overcome sin. Therefore, a Savior was needed. The Jews call Him "the Messiah" (*ha Messhiach*). Christians know him as "the Christ" (Jesus of Nazareth).

Romans 7:15

> For that which I do I allow not: for what I would, that do I not; but what I hate, that do I.

Paul wrote this chapter to those who knew what it was to live under the Law. He uses the pronoun *I* to include all mankind. Any person under the Law finds himself doing what is against his own standards, as found in the Law. He wants to do everything righteously, but he fails. The things he detests doing are the very things he finds himself doing. He is overcome by sin; often when he least expects it.

We will recognize our own lifestyle described here if we have the Ten Commandments or church laws as our way to righteousness. This is our way of life if we use one or all of them as a way for righteous living.

In one sentence we can now say: that everyone under the written Law breaks it, even though it is against their own will. It happens even under civil law. Check yourself out by seeing how many times you break traffic laws, even against your own will!

Paul, who grew up under the Law, experienced Romans 7:15 for himself. In 1 Timothy 1:15–16, he declares, "I was the worst of sinners... before I was converted."

Some theologians hint that Paul's teaching on the danger

of the Law is his own theory—that it is not in agreement with other parts of the New Testament. However, Paul writes:

> But I certify you, brethren, that the gospel which was preached of me is not after man. For I neither received it of man, neither was I taught it, but by the revelation of Jesus Christ...Now the things which I write unto you, behold, before God, I lie not.
>
> —Galatians 1:11–12, 20

Are we leading lives of constant defeat, as described above in Romans 7:15, or are we overcomers, walking by faith as new men and women of God, in righteousness and true holiness? Are we dead to sin and sinning and alive to God in Christ Jesus? Is it no longer self doing the living, but Christ who lives in us? Are we openly confessing the truth that we were once slaves to sin but now, thank God, are slaves to righteousness?

Christian, if your lifestyle agrees with Romans 7:15, the Law has a hold on your life, and you have turned off the flow of God's grace and righteousness. You will therefore not receive your eternal inheritance on that day, unless you change. We are eternally saved by grace, by obeying the Spirit of grace.

Paul writes in Galatians 3:11, "No man is justified by the law in the sight of God." Now we can understand why he told the Corinthian church, "...the letter [Law] killeth" (2 Cor. 3:6).

Or as Paul says in Galatians 2:21, "Do not frustrate the grace of God [do not turn it off]" by the Law. The Law aborts the power of the cross.

> ...except your righteousness shall exceed the righteousness of the scribes and Pharisees, ye shall in no case enter into the kingdom of heaven.
>
> —Matthew 5:20

Chapter 21

The Law of Sin

ROMANS 7:16–17 SAYS:

> If then I do that which I would not, I consent unto the law that it is good. Now then it is no more I that do it, but sin that dwelleth in me.

Paul has at last exposed the culprit. It is a power for evil. It lives in my flesh, and it is in rebellion against God. Its name is *sin*. Paul says later that no good thing lives in flesh.

My human nature was made perfect, but sin took control of it and perverted it. Therefore, only a fool would embrace anything that gives power to this rebellion called sin. Since the coming of Christ, only a fool—or a person who is deceived—embraces the Law of Commandments.

It is crucial that we grasp the truth that we are not the culprits. No! We are only the slaves under the slave master, sin. Of course, Paul has previously shown in chapter 6 that Jesus freed us from sin's control by taking us to death on His cross. His death set us free in our baptism into Jesus Christ.

Therefore, I know without question that Paul is here describing the condition of a person who is under the Law and excluded from the grace that flows from the cross by the Holy Spirit of grace. He *is not* describing the condition of a born-of-the-Spirit, Spirit-led son of God.

Satan is very happy for us to accept the false notion of Bible teachers who erroneously declare Romans 7 to be a description of a true Christian lifestyle. He knows that we are deceived and defeated once we believe and confess that it is normal to continue sinning.

However, Christ is calling us to come apart from this great deception. It is a heart-wrenching decision, and it will be followed by persecution. But if we remain where we are in the Law—and therefore sinning—we cannot expect our inheritance. We have cut off our supply of grace, without which no man can be saved.

Satan is very pleased and contented when he sees Christians embracing the Ten Commandments for righteousness. He knows that they are under the law of sin and therefore are his, for "he that committeth sin is of the devil" (1 John 3:8). This is why Jesus said to the church leaders who taught the Law, "Your father is the devil" (John 8:44).

Romans 7 clearly teaches that all who are under the Law are sinners. It follows that they are under the devil because anyone who sins is of the devil.

Praise God that we who are baptized into Christ's death are, ourselves, dead to sin and dead to the Law. But we must accept it by faith, confess it, and walk in it. This is the new man of God.

ROMANS 7:18

> For I know that in me (that is, in my flesh,) dwelleth no good thing: for to will is present with me; but how to perform that which is good I find not.

The "no good thing" that lives in our flesh is sin.

- Can we overcome it? *Impossible!*
- Will the Law help? *No!*
- What about prayer, fasting, and determination? *No good!*

Nothing, absolutely nothing we try, can overcome the power of sin. It forces us to commit sins even against our strongest will. The only way to get away from sin is for the flesh itself to die.

Do you now understand why Jesus took us to death in His death? Accept your co-death with Jesus, confess it, and you are freed from sin's power. Our old man died on Calvary's cross; therefore by faith, put on the new man of God. We are dead to sin and alive to God.

Two thousand years have rolled by and about forty-two generations have passed away since Paul penned Romans 7. But most of the church is still trying to avoid sinning by willpower, works, or the Law. It is mixing flesh with Spirit, and it cannot succeed. Galatians 5:17 teaches that the flesh, because of sin, is in a running battle against the Spirit of God. As Genesis 3:6 shows, the flesh demands the knowledge of good and evil. It wants more and more knowledge so that self can claim some glory.

The church has been beset by the flesh and its world system for two thousand years. As a result, the morality of both the church and the world has grown worse and worse until today, when we are faced with an ugly monster of our own making—a monster that is out of control.

Paul's explanation that sin is the master over the flesh-man needs to be understood and accepted by the church. Then we will be able to know how to throw back the enemy. We need to be like little children and just believe the Scripture of the New Testament and "do it." To defeat our enemy, we must forsake the Law and accept God's grace of freedom from sin in Christ Jesus.

We insult God's grace when we accept forgiveness but reject freedom. Sadly, only a tiny remnant of "the called of God" reckon their flesh dead to sin and alive to God in Christ. Only a few confess their belief in the scriptural truth that they are dead to the written Law and to sin and are leading a righteous (sinless) lifestyle by abiding in Christ. Only a small number are walking by faith in the law of the Spirit of life in Christ Jesus, set free from the law of sinning and immediate spiritual death.

Only a few understand that Romans 7 describes the self-righteous lifestyle (also identified in Romans 10:1–4) of the unregenerate sinner and the Christian who is under the Law. Both are defeated. They are dead and are going to the second death.

ROMANS 7:19

> For the good that I would I do not: but the evil which I would not, that I do.

Paul is repeating his statement in verse 15 to establish a second witness of Scripture and to again drive home the importance of knowing exactly what he is explaining. Romans 7 is not about our future rank in heaven; it is about getting into heaven.

We see here the confusion and frustration in the mind of a flesh-man. I do not come across many Christians who do not agree that verse 19 sums up their own lifestyle.

How did we ever get it so wrong? We have perverted

Romans 7 imagining it to be a description of the normal Christian life. But we walk by sight and not by Scripture. Therefore, we do not understand that Romans 7 is about the condition of fallen mankind—dominated by sin, which is empowered by Law.

Mention in Christian circles that you are walking sinlessly (righteously), and you will see an immediate manifestation of demons. Of course, Satan's gang is determined always to fight tooth and nail against Christ's promise (in John 8:34 and 36 that He sets us free from committing sins). However, Satan is in disarray and flees from a foe who is armed with a true understanding of, and faith in, Romans 6–8 and 1 John 3.

Being perfect and being sinless are two separate things. The rich young man who came to Jesus and was seeking perfection claimed that he was sinless as far as the Law was concerned. Jesus accepted his claim and told him, "You have established the correct base, but to become perfect, you must forsake all and follow me."

Perfection pertains to people who first possess a righteous lifestyle and continue on to the virtues of the stature of Christ. I need to be living righteously to be accepted into heaven. My degree of perfection is what will determine my position in heaven. Being a Christian is about sinless people striving in the Spirit to reach perfection.

Dear Reader, failing to understand that sinlessness and perfection are two separate things will result in confusion, which prevents us from understanding the New Testament Scripture.

> For whom he did foreknow, he also did predestinate to be conformed to the image of his Son.
>
> —Romans 8:29

The Christian lifestyle is about sinless-living saints being perfected. Ephesians 4:13 says:

> Till we all come in the unity of the faith, and of the knowledge of the Son of God, unto a perfect man, unto the measure of the stature of the fulness of Christ.

The Christian lifestyle is not about struggling to overcome sin. We become Christians by being born of the Spirit of God, and, according to 1 John 3:9, anyone born of God cannot sin. Anyone walking by faith in the Spirit of God cannot sin, "for the law of the Spirit of life in Christ Jesus hath made me free from the law of sin and death" (Rom. 8:2).

It is a walk of faith in Christ and His promises from start to finish, for the just shall *live* by faith. We are born again because of our faith in Christ Jesus, and we proceed along the path of perfection by our faith in Christ Jesus. Only unbelief and willful sinning, described in Hebrews 10:26–31, will bar us from entering heaven.

Our degree of perfection is directly related to our detachment from the world (worldly: brethren, friends and relatives, worldly dignity and prudence, money and possessions, and affairs of the world). We must be attached to friendship with Jesus—in love with Him through His Spirit.

Romans 7:20

> Now if I do that I would not, it is no more I that do it, but sin that dwelleth in me.

Paul, being well aware that new information needs repeating to penetrate an old mind-set, challenges us again with verse 20. Have we really accepted the fact that sin, this force for evil, controlled us before we gave up the Law and began to walk in the Spirit? When we accept this, we discover that the world, the flesh, and the devil can do nothing but tempt us. We committed sins because this thing called *sin* actually forced us to do it.

At last, we are having our enemy identified. I always thought it was my nature. But now I see that my nature is good, for I am made in God's image. No, it is not our nature that is evil. It is this enemy, sin, which twists our good nature to do evil. Sin controls people who are under the Law. This is why the Scripture emphasizes that our Savior came to defeat the sin of the world. Please study this for yourself in 1 John 3:8.

Dear Reader, be aware that there is a world of difference between the eye reading something and the mind understanding it. Please take time to absorb what Paul is teaching us in these verses, for it concerns our future inheritance, our eternal salvation, our eternal life.

Romans 7:21

> I find then a law, that, when I would do good, evil is present with me.

Paul speaks here about discovering another law. Laws always originate from a person or body of people who hold authority. Nobody can change them except the people who made them. The rules that govern the universe are called laws because nobody can change them. Scientists and scholars understand these laws and recognize that that they operate, whether we like it or not. They know that disobeying or simply ignoring these laws brings disaster.

For example, the designer of every building must design it in accordance with the law of gravity, which was discovered by Isaac Newton, but decreed by God. Every mechanical action undertaken by man, from walking to flying, is done in accordance with the law of gravity. Water and air are under its control.

Therefore, Paul recognizes by way of observation and a revelation from Jesus Christ that sinning is an inescapable rule of life for natural mankind. He declares it to be a law. Natural man can no more escape being a sinner than he can escape the law of gravity. Mankind is born under the law of sin.

A man may jump high above his own head into the air, but he cannot escape a quick return to earth under the law of gravity. Likewise a man can make a choice to resist every temptation to commit sins, but the law of sin will always have the last say and cause him to fall.

It is crucial for us to understand that the law of sin is not the law of God that was written by Him on stone tablets. Paul writes about these two different laws in a way that most misunderstand, and it results in confusion and dire consequences. However, I have found that if we stick to the words of the Bible, it eliminates most errors of interpretation—errors that have led so many times to the establishment of yet another denomination or sect.

If we do not understand the law of sin, we will never understand chapters 7 and 8 of Paul's epistle to the Romans and to us. You see, Paul introduces us to a third law in Romans 8:2.

Some call the law of sin our *human nature,* but the Bible does not. Natural human nature is not evil, but good. *The law of sin, which controls human nature, is evil.* Paul has written six chapters in the Book of Romans as a lead-up to our understanding that the natural man is under the law of sin. Until we fully understand and agree with this, we will never comprehend the mercy of God's grace.

Hebrews 9:7 teaches that under the old covenant of God's written laws, sins that were not willful could be forgiven. The new covenant is not new with regard to forgiveness. It is new because it sets man free from further sinning. This is what the apostles called *the good news.*

Romans 7:22

For I delight in the law of God after the inward man.

All sincere Christians and Jews recognize with their mind that the written laws of God are good. But:

Romans 7:23

> I see another law in my members, warring against the law of my mind, and bringing me into captivity to the law of sin which is in my members.

Sin is a law that lives in the members of a living body and forces unredeemed man to commit sins. It operates through our five senses. Previously Paul wrote that his own unredeemed man [the old man] is dead. Therefore, we know without doubt that Paul uses the personal pronoun *I* and the present tense in this chapter to emphasize that he is not writing about himself.

Instead, he is writing to any *carnal* readers of his letter so they will realize that the law of sin is the ongoing personal problem of unredeemed mankind. Step by step, he is describing the lifestyle of the lost. He does so until they finally call out, "You are so right, man. That's me to a tee; that's my lifestyle exactly. I try each day to do right but know deep down there will be sinful failures." Once he has them at the point of recognizing that they are trapped, he then proceeds to give them the means of being set free for life.

When I talk to Christians, 99.9 percent of them say that they certainly think Paul is describing their own life and the typical Christian lifestyle in chapter 7. They even think, mistakenly, that he is describing his own life as an apostle. I believe their eyes and understanding have been blinded to Paul's words that follow from verse 23 and into chapter 8.

These Christians are carnal and living in the realm of sight, not faith. Could they be trusting in their past experiences and teachers instead of walking by faith in Christ's promises? Certainly they are misunderstanding Paul's teaching in Romans 6 and 7. Second Peter 3:16 warns about "unlearned and unstable [Christians who] wrest… [Paul's] scriptures, unto their own destruction."

Peter says that all of Paul's epistles teach us to avoid

destruction and "be diligent that ye may be found of him in peace, without spot, and blameless" (2 Pet. 3:14). I say, *God help the typical Christian who is living the blameable lifestyle of Romans 7.* I believe Peter uses the word *destruction* as a euphemism. He is writing as gently as possible about the eternal lake of fire—the second death.

To those who are under the law of sin, I point you again to Paul's fellow apostle Peter, who writes in Scripture:

> Beware lest ye also, being led away with the error of the wicked, fall from your own stedfastness. But grow in grace, and [in] the knowledge of our Lord and Saviour Jesus Christ.
>
> —2 PETER 3:17–18

I see it in my garden every day. The plant that is not growing is dying! Often pruning will save it. Pruning is painful. But even though it hurts to admit that we are on the wrong track, I encourage you with all my heart to change and walk the path of victory instead of the one that leads to destruction.

I, like Paul, had to admit that I had it wrong when I had been a "Christian" nearly fifty years. But I allowed God's grace to open my eyes. I accepted in faith that Christ had set me free from the law of sin, and it worked!

When God said, "I will never leave thee, nor forsake thee" He was speaking to people who step out every day with faith in Him and His promises. In 2 Chronicles 15:1–2, Azariah spoke a prophecy to Asa, the king of Judah:

> The LORD is with you, while ye be with him; and if ye seek him, he will be found of you; but if ye forsake him, he will forsake you.

These words remain true forever. As Hebrews 10:26 teaches, "If we sin wilfully after that we have received the knowledge of the truth, there remaineth no more sacrifice for sins."

Satan sets a trap for Christians to think, *Well I can't be perfect anyway. So what if I sin a little? God will forgive me.* Satan told Eve, "[You] shall not surely die" if you eat of the tree of knowledge of good and evil (Gen. 2:16–17, 3:1–4). But she did die. She had received the knowledge of the truth from the mouth of God, via her husband, but she was tricked into willful sinning. There remained no forgiveness; she was driven out of paradise and prevented from reentry.

It is an example for us converted Christians, so that we too do not again become deceived by Satan and lose our eternal salvation (eternal life). I became as Adam and Eve on the day I believed and was reconciled to God as a friend. But Satan is out to get me again!

Romans 7:24–25

> O wretched man that I am! who shall deliver me from the body of this death? I thank God through Jesus Christ our Lord. So then with the mind I myself serve the law of God; but with the flesh the law of sin.

In chapter 7, Paul has painted a picture that shows the lifestyle of a Christian or Jew who is walking according to the dictates of the sinful flesh. Both are still under the written Law and are trying desperately to obey it. However, they cannot, because their sinful flesh has not been put to death by faith in Christ's promise. Therefore, their sinful bodies have them in the grip of spiritual death. They are physically alive and walk around, but on the inside, they are spiritually dead.

Religion may tell them that they are not dead, but deep down, they do not feel easy. They try religion, but find that it does not work. Paul identifies himself with them because he himself was once an exemplary religious Jew. As far as the Law was concerned, he says in Philippians 3:6, he was "blameless." Yet at the same time, he says in 1 Timothy 1:15–16, that he was "chief" among sinners before he "obtained [Christ's] mercy."

On behalf of all religious people he cries out, "Who shall deliver me from this sinful body of mine, which causes me to sin and therefore be spiritually dead?" He then gives God's perfect answer, "I thank God through Jesus Christ, the One who delivers me from sin and death!"

You may be thinking, *But I gave my life to Christ and went into baptism. I follow my Christian religion as best I can, and I am humble enough to admit that I am still sinning (a little). Anyway, I trust in my own interpretation of 1 John 1:9.*

Well, my friend, Paul is not finished yet. The best is coming. Soon, he is going to explain what living the Christian life is all about. It's about reaching for the stars! It's about seeking "those things which are above, where Christ sitteth on the right hand of God" (Col. 3:1). It does not mean that we merely start to follow Christ. No! We also identify with Him. We become part of Him.

Paul mentioned in chapter 5 that we are to be saved by His life. He was writing about Christ actually living inside us and directing our lives, keeping us righteous, so that we can inherit eternal life. He wrote to the Christians in Galatia:

> I am crucified with Christ [died with Jesus]: nevertheless I live; yet not I, but Christ liveth in me: and the life which I now live in the flesh I live by the faith of the Son of God, who loved me, and gave himself for me. I do not frustrate the grace of God: for if righteousness [come] by the law, then Christ is dead in vain.
>
> —GALATIANS 2:20–21

There is only one way to be eternally saved at our judgment. It is by having a righteous (blameless) lifestyle—a life of faith in the promise that each day we live not our own way, but after the leading of the indwelling Christ. It is no longer we who live, but Christ who lives in us. We live by His grace (Gal. 2:22).

Without holiness no man will see God (Heb. 12:14). Your initial reconciliation (salvation) is by faith alone (Rom. 10:9) but our eternal salvation is by faith working through love (Gal. 5:6; Heb. 10:26–31; 1 Pet. 1:16; Rom. 8:2, 4).

If we are living with the religious, lukewarm, split personality of being a saint and yet a sinner (a spiritual schizophrenic), Paul shows us the way out of this dilemma in chapter 8. But it means that we will have to stop playing church and get real!

It is impossible to get real if we still mistakenly believe that Paul is describing himself as being in a sinful-saved condition in chapter 7. If Paul were truly writing that he is still under the control of the law of sin, he would be contradicting himself. In chapter 6, he declared that baptized believers are dead to sin and have become slaves to righteousness. He said that our body of sin was destroyed when our old man was crucified with Christ "that henceforth we [should] not serve sin" (Rom. 6:6).

Paul also said that he was dead to the Law of Moses, which gives power to sin. If Paul is contradicting himself, it follows that we can discard the New Testament as a farce and toss it out with the rubbish of the world. Of course, Paul is not a fool and is recognized by the intelligentsia of the world as one of the world's greatest teachers. The church itself has declared for two thousand years that all of his writings are scripturally sound and inspired by God.

No, the trouble is not with Paul. The trouble is with those who do not believe Paul. They cannot accept by faith that the old, carnal man is dead, and they therefore continue to commit sins. They say, "I did not actually die with Jesus; it was just a spiritual sort of death." Or they teach that it means "as if I were dead." Ken Taylor's well-known and widely accepted paraphrase of the New Testament waters it down to "…so you died with him so to speak." This indicates that perhaps our old man did not actually die and was not actually buried. But Paul says that we did die, and we were buried with Him.

My dear reader, I have been studying Romans chapters 6–8

for thirty years, and I can assure you that Paul's words are not to be diminished. He received each word from God, and changing a word can change the meaning of the entire teaching.

I agree that believing that we died is a hard saying and impossible to understand. *But* if I do not accept it by faith, because it is the Word of God, it profits me nothing. I am rejecting God's promise that my old man, my carnal body, died at Calvary. Now if my old man did not actually die, I have to continue battling with him. It always follows that if we doubt God's Word, nothing changes. As Galatians 5:6 says, nothing avails "but faith which worketh by love."

Not believing that we actually died and were buried with Christ quite logically leads us to believe that we are still in a constant war with the old man of sinful flesh, as Paul describes in Romans 7. It's no wonder that Christians are ashamed to say they are no longer sinning. We have swallowed Satan's bait and altered the meaning of the scripture that declares our sinful flesh actually died. Satan has hooked us. But Scripture is emphatic—only dead men are freed from sin.

Believe me, Satan will continue to hold us in the grip of sin if we are not believing and confessing the truth of Romans 6:6-11 that our carnal body is dead. Does a butterfly still look as if the old grub has not died? Does the blade of wheat look like its seed grain did not die in the ground? These are God-given, living parables if we have eyes to see them.

We may continue to hold out against our death by asking, "Why does Paul use the pronoun *I* and the present tense when describing the carnal Christian in chapter 7, if he were not in that state himself?" Before I answer that question, I want to remind you that a carnal Christian who is still under the law of sin cannot shake himself free from sinning. He cannot believe that the old, carnal man is dead. Therefore he does not receive the benefit of death. All mankind is reconciled to God at the cross, but people who do not believe it do not receive the benefit of being reconciled.

Paul is writing under instruction from the Holy Spirit. To emphasize that he himself knows from experience what he writes is true, he uses a method well-known to the ancient teachers. He inserts *I* instead of *you* or *they* and writes in the present tense. In this way, he makes the teaching more lively and acceptable and hopefully ensures that it is readily understood by the one who is a guilty pupil. The known risk is that the unlearned and the doubters will imagine that the teacher himself is still guilty too.

I suffered with asthma for forty-five years before I was miraculously and permanently healed by the Holy Spirit of Jesus Christ thirty years ago. Now, when I talk to asthmatics, I emphasize that I have been there myself by using the personal pronoun *I* and saying things that describe a typical asthmatic. For example, I may say, "As an asthmatic, I cannot go to bed on a full stomach without starting to wheeze; neither can I get overtired, run down, or overexcited." If they were not listening to my explanation of having been healed, they would mistakenly think that I am still suffering with asthma and severely restricted.

Similarly, Paul spent the whole of chapter 6 and the beginning of chapter 7 explaining that he was already freed from sin. But if we have not been paying attention to what the Lord is saying to us, through Paul, we will mistakenly think that Paul is still bound by the law of sin. Satan is always around to suggest that it is more sensible to follow sight and our own understanding than to have complete faith in God's promises.

That old dragon appears to have been very successful in deceiving the church into believing that Paul and all born-of-the-Spirit Christians are still in combat with their master, the law of sin.

Personally, I follow Paul's teaching that he is free, just as Jesus taught we would be in John 8:36. Galatians 2:20 teaches:

> I am crucified with Christ: nevertheless I live; yet not I, but Christ liveth in me: and the life which I now live in

> the flesh I live by the faith of the Son of God, who loved me, and gave himself for me.

I believe this, and confessing my belief turns it into faith, without which I cannot please God, according to Hebrews 11:6. As a result, I find in Romans 6:11 that I am truly dead to sin and alive to God in Christ Jesus.

> But the Comforter, which is the Holy Ghost, whom the Father will send in my name, he shall teach you all things, and bring all things to your remembrance, whatsoever I [Jesus] have said unto you.
>
> —JOHN 14:26

Chapter 22

Race to Win

Paul is now ready to show us how to walk in our new freedom from sin. It is not about fighting or about choosing. It is about faith and a victorious lifestyle.

Are we ready for the victory race? *Do we want to race to win?* Or are we like the Christians in Frank Peretti's book *The Oath?*[1] In a thrilling story, he pictures sin as a dragon and a Christian as the dragon hunter, armed with a suitable dragon-killing gun. After an unbelievably difficult chase through mountains and subterranean caves, the hunter finally corners the dragon. There is no escape. Getting him in his sights, he prepares to shoot at point blank range.

However, slowly but surely, the hunter starts to lower the barrel until it is pointing at the ground. When it came to the pinch, he just did not have the heart to kill sin. Peretti is a deep-thinking man, and I believe that the hunter with the gun represents the church of our day.

Why, when it comes to the crunch, do we not want to eliminate sinning? Is it because we would lose our claim to humility or our claim to humanity? Is it our unbelief that sinning actually kills us, or fear of ridicule or the end of our counseling work? Maybe it's the fact that we really prefer to "look normal" and walk by sight instead of by faith.

One of our beloved brothers recently wrote a large scholarly and scriptural book on the subject of being freed from sin. But he shot himself in the foot by concluding emphatically that every Christian is going to commit sin even after they believe that Christ has set them free. I find no New Testament scripture that states or implies Christians will commit sin again.

Children play a game called "Let's Pretend." It may be, "Let's pretend we are cowboys and Indians...or kings and queens." Perhaps as adults, we mistake "Let's Pretend" for faith. We do not want to disobey the Scriptures, so we decide to believe that we died with Christ. But is it really a case of pretending that we died with Christ.

Deep down, we think that if it sets us free from sin, we will then be able to believe it. This, of course, does not work because "without faith it is impossible to please [God]" (Heb. 11:6). We forget that we have to first get out of the boat if we are going to walk on water. Faith does not figure it out beforehand.

Church history reveals that the Holy Spirit often brings a wave of revival. And before long, a subtle antirevival takes place and sweeps away the life of the Spirit. Our let's-pretend faith soon dries up, and we revive the old man who is controlled by doubt and sin. The game of "Let's Pretend" is too unreal to be lasting. Only true faith brings lasting reality to our own life and the life of the church.

Without a faith that starts from deep-down belief and wells up through our mouths and into our actions, we will never reap the benefits of our being dead to sin and dead to the Law of written commandments. Without a living faith, we will always remain slaves to sin. But we will wind up in the lake of fire because we have rejected God's grace.

The beset-by-sinning church of our day is a witness to the truths I am writing. Many profess that they know God, "but in works they deny him, being abominable, and disobedient, and unto every good work reprobate" (Titus 1:16). Good works are actions and deeds initiated by God's love. The Bible clearly teaches that we cannot be reconciled to God by our works.

But just as surely, it teaches that "the reconciled man," the new-creation man, will be judged on his works:

> For we must all appear before the judgment seat of Christ; that every one may receive the things done in his body, according to that he hath done, whether [it be] good or bad.
>
> —2 Corinthians 5:10

First Peter 1:17 says that God judges every man according to their works, and teaches us to pass our time here on earth in fear. God finds out who we really are by examining what we have done.

It is of no use to read what comes next in Paul's letter to the Romans if we have not accepted, without reserve, that a person has to be dead to sin *before* he can be alive to God. I am, as a human being, born a slave to sin until death. I died when I accepted that I died with Christ.

Now Paul is going to teach us how to stay free in our new life in Christ. If we are careless, we can find ourselves back under our old master, sin. Paul, being an eminent teacher who was trained by the highly respected Gamaliel ("a doctor of the law" identified in Acts 5:34), already has hinted several times about our new life which can come once we have died.

- Romans 5:10: "For if, when we were enemies, we were reconciled to God by the death of his Son, much more, being reconciled, we shall be saved by his life." Paul wrote of the lifestyle by which we will be saved at the judgment, a lifestyle of obeying the Spirit of God's Son.

- Romans 6:4: "That like as Christ was raised up from the dead...even so we also should walk in newness of life."

- Romans 6:8: "Since we are dead with Christ, we believe that we shall also *live* with him."

- Romans 7:6: "But now we are delivered from the law [of written commandments], that being dead wherein we were held; that we should serve in newness of spirit, and not in the oldness of the letter."

- Romans 7:24–25: "O wretched man that I am! who shall deliver me from the body of this death? I thank God—through Jesus Christ our Lord."

For the eyes of the Lord are over the righteous, and his ears are open unto *their* prayers: but the face of the Lord is against them that do evil.

—1 Peter 3:12

Chapter 23

Romans 8

In Romans 8, Paul explains that since Christians have become dead to sin and the written Law, they can now live a righteous life, free from the law of sin. Because he was a Jew, he well knew the prophecy of Daniel 9:24, that the Messiah—Christ—would set His people free from sinning. Romans 8 is simply a confirmation that this prophecy had been fulfilled and would operate in the life of any Spirit-filled Christian who believes it is true. It logically sets out a detailed description of why and how we live the sinless, righteous life of being led by the Spirit of Christ Jesus.

Being sinless, we cannot be condemned, says Paul. Romans 8:1–2 begins by telling us we cannot be condemned:

> There is therefore now no condemnation to them which are in Christ Jesus, who walk not after the flesh, but after the Spirit. For the law of the Spirit of life in Christ Jesus hath made me free from the law of sin and death.

Therefore, we look forward with God's hope for our salvation when He returns. Romans 8:24 says, "For we are saved by hope: but hope that is seen is not hope: for what a man seeth, why doth he yet hope for?"

Paul concludes Romans 8 with the majestic and awesome promise of a sovereign and loving God. These latter verses reveal that people who walk in the Spirit of Christ are not only freed from sin, but are also predestined and called to conform to the image of God's Son—their own brother, Jesus. They will be glorified one day. Paul finishes the chapter on the note that all things work together for their good and that they cannot be separated from His love.

Chapter 24

Not Condemned—Why Not?

Romans 8:1–2 says:

> There is therefore now no condemnation to them which are in Christ Jesus, who walk not after the flesh, but after the Spirit. For the law of the Spirit of life in Christ Jesus hath made me free from the law of sin and death.

We have died to the Law of Commandments and to the law of sin. Here Paul introduces the replacement law—the law of the Spirit of life in Christ Jesus. This is the life that, according to Romans 6:4 and 8:11, Jesus received from the Holy Spirit when He raised Jesus from the dead.

I was given that life in my personal Pentecost experience

when I received from Jesus the baptism of the Holy Spirit. I find that my new life in the Spirit is a real, new, and wonderful experience that changes my whole lifestyle. It changes my way of thinking and shatters all my wrong mind-sets. My life under sin was like an ugly earthbound grub. But now my life in His Spirit is like a beautiful, free-roaming butterfly!

Any believer is eligible to receive the Holy Spirit; but sadly, many (who once included me) are not open to receive Him. This may be because of ignorance or a fear of manifesting His presence in ways that are frowned on by religious leaders. I was afraid of losing my worldly dignity.

In the Book of Acts, the giving and receiving of the Holy Spirit is always accompanied by some manifestation of the new-life experience. Jesus defined it as being "born of the Spirit" (John 3:6). John called it "born of God" in 1 John 3:9 and said that the great change He brings is that the person can no longer commit sins.

I thank God that in my lifetime there has been a real Latter Rain outpouring of the Holy Spirit in response to a worldwide hunger and thirsting for His experiential presence within. It is what God promised His people in Acts 1:4 and 2:39. John 1:13 explains that we cannot be born of God and enter into new life by our own will or desire, for it depends on God's will.

Paul calls this *new life* a power that has made us free from the law of sin and death. By the indwelling Spirit of Jesus Christ, we are no longer living under the rule of sin. Nevertheless, like Adam and Eve, if we disobey the Spirit, we will become outcasts and lose our inheritance. We will be back under Satan's law of sin. In 1 Corinthians 9:27, Paul warns us to keep our flesh-body under control, lest we become outcasts.

Paul, of course, is writing to Spirit-filled Christians. He later points out that until we receive the Holy Spirit we are not Christians at all. In Romans 8:9, he says, "Now if any man have not the Spirit of Christ, he is none of his."

Personally, I consider Romans 8:1–2 to be the most wonderful verse in the whole New Testament. It assures me that my faith has placed me in Christ Jesus, and, therefore, because I am no longer sinning, I cannot be condemned.

The *Jerusalem Bible* paraphrases and clarifies the meaning of Romans 8:1–2 in these words: "The reason therefore, why those in Christ Jesus are not condemned, is that the law of the Spirit of life in Christ Jesus has set you free from the law of sin and death."

Thank God, it is no longer a case of trying to make a choice between right and wrong, a choice which no man can make unerringly. For now it is simply a walk of faith and obedience to the Spirit of Christ. This is a walk that operates under the unchangeable law of my freedom from sin and its punishment, death.

Praise the Lord! At last I have a sinless life through my faith in the life-giving power of Christ's Spirit! As Galatians 2:20 says, it is truly no longer I who live, but Christ who lives in me. The old man is dead and buried, according to Romans 6:4. Second Corinthians 5:17 teaches that I am new creation, and I am thrilled!

Being a Christian is not about us making choices. It is about us being obedient to the Good Shepherd. This is God's amazing grace in action. Paul assures us that our battle with sinful flesh is finished if we will believe it and confess it. Without sin controlling our flesh, it is easy to keep our flesh under control and obey only the desires of the Holy Spirit. We are no longer the old carnal, sinful people, who, as Romans 7:15–23 describes, waged continual and unsuccessful war against sin and sinning when we were under the Law of commandments and the law of sin.

No! We have put on the new man of God, created in righteousness and true holiness. We are no longer sinners pretending to be saints. We have become true saints, who no longer sin, for that is the meaning of the word *saint*. Instead of being controlled by the sinful flesh, we are controlled by the Spirit of God from within; for out of our innermost being flows the water of life—eternal life—as Jesus promised in John 7:38–39.

I do not pay any attention to teachers who keep insisting that I am still a sinner but saved by grace. I am now a new creation, part of what 1 Peter 2:9 calls "a chosen generation, a royal priesthood, an holy nation, a peculiar people... [called by God] out of darkness into his marvelous light." This is how grace saves me. I am "saved by His life" for eternal life, according to Romans 5:10. I do not call myself a sinning sinner and thereby, as Hebrews 10:26-31 warns, insult the Spirit of grace.

Summing up verses 1–2 of Romans 8, we can say that it contains God's promise of divine justice on Judgment Day. For the saints set free from sinning, there is no condemnation; for the ones who refused God's grace and continued in sin, there will be condemnation.

Romans 8:3

> For what the law could not do, in that it was weak through the flesh, God sending his own Son in the likeness of sinful flesh, and for sin, condemned sin in the flesh.

Jesus Christ did not come the first time to condemn anyone. He came to condemn sin by taking our sinful flesh to death and exchanging it with flesh that is not sinful.

No longer does sin, the cruel taskmaster, rule us. We are now ruled by the love of Christ, by His Spirit in our spirit. We have the mind of Christ, a spiritual mind. The Holy Spirit in the human spirit rules and keeps us righteous. It all takes place by our active faith in the promises of Christ.

The Law of Commandments can never condemn sin and cannot make us righteous. On the contrary, the Law condemns us. As Paul says in Romans 10:4, "Christ is the end of the law for righteousness to every one that believeth."

Therefore, we must not seek to go back to our roots. It can add nothing to Christ.

Romans 8:4

> That the righteousness of the law might be fulfilled in us, who walk not after the flesh, but after the Spirit.

God's people had spent fourteen long centuries attempting to be righteous by the Law. They failed, "for all have sinned, and come short of the glory of God" (Rom. 3:23). They were all sinners. The Messiah, Jesus Christ, came on the scene and set them free from the Law and free from sin. He made available to everyone a sinless, righteous lifestyle. We fulfil all of God's law by trusting Him to run our lives. It's our faith accepting His grace!

He did not come to do away with the Law; He came to fulfill it, as Matthew 5:17–18 teaches. In Him, we fulfill every tittle of it. The Law is fulfilled by love, according to Romans 13:10, and 1 John 4:8 declares, "God is love." By walking in the Holy Spirit's love, we automatically fulfill the Law.

The battle is over. For the saints, there is no more war every day, just faith working through love. We're on the victory march!

I do not give my sin-free flesh any chance to fall for temptations again. I do not indulge it, but I keep it under and walk by faith through deeds of love. If I grow slack, I will become a castaway, and my last state will be worse than my first. I am perfectly safe on the narrow road, but if I veer to the left or to the right, I will disappear down into the abyss of darkness.

Romans 8:5

> For they that are after the flesh do mind the things of the flesh; but they that are after the Spirit the things of the Spirit.

Even though my flesh is no longer under the control of sin, it still is easily drawn into demanding excesses. Flesh is the point of mankind's temptations to commit sins. Without flesh, I cannot sin. Therefore, like Jesus, I do not obey any demands of my flesh, unless the Holy Spirit leads me to do so.

The Holy Spirit never allows the flesh to obey temptations to commit sins. Eve's flesh was not under the control of sin, but by disobeying the Spirit of God, she fell for the temptation that appealed to her flesh. From then on, she was under the power of sin. Her inner man had died. As Romans 6:23 says, "The wages of sin is death." God's law demands it!

I make sure I do not follow the pattern of the Fall of Adam and Eve. *In* Christ, I am a new Adam, who never falls unless I disobey the leading of the Spirit. Notice that I did not say "is never tempted."

Romans 8:6

> For to be carnally minded is death; but to be spiritually minded is life and peace.

If we are going to have a new lifestyle (of life and peace) under the direction and care of the Holy Spirit, we must first accept the promise that we died with Christ when we first believed. Therefore, we are dead to sin and dead to that which gives power to sin—the Law of Commandments. Nevertheless we still have bodies of flesh and blood. Our bodies are no longer under the control of sin, but they are the place where we are tempted to commit sins.

Jesus had a body in the likeness of sinful flesh, but He was not under the control of sin. Yet, Satan tempted Him to commit sins by appealing to His flesh. Because Jesus was walking in the Spirit, He was able to resist the devil. Jesus did not allow His mind to make decisions based on the signals He received from the five senses. His mind was submitted to the signals that came from His Father via the Holy Spirit within.

The Scriptures state that Jesus was a Man like us in all things except sin and sinning. He "was in all points tempted like as we are, yet without sin" (Heb. 4:15). As 1 Peter 2:22 says, He "did no sin, neither was guile found in his mouth."

It follows that since it is no longer I who live, but Christ who lives in me, I too am now a flesh and blood man freed from the power of sin and sinning. I do it all by faith in Christ and His promises. Christ is called the second Adam because the first Adam was also a flesh-and-blood man free from the control of sin until his faith in God's promise turned to doubt. Doubting God is a sin, and it led Adam to disobedience and falling for the temptation of the devil, through his wife. The temptation was to indulge himself in the knowledge of God's law. That sinning took him to instant spiritual death. In Christ, we too are second Adams. If we walk by faith according to the Spirit, we will have Spirit-of-God minds.

If, however, we listen to our flesh, we will have carnal flesh-minds. Flesh-minds are unable to resist the cunning wiles of Satan and will irrevocably fall under temptation. This will cause us to be trapped again by sin and death, as was the first Adam.

Before conversion, we have no possible way of overcoming every temptation to commit sins. But after the conversion of spiritual rebirth, we are new creations; second-Adam people who are able to walk, by faith, the sinless walk of Christ. We have no reason to boast, for it is not by our own choosing but by the grace of the sinless Christ and His faith given to us by the Holy Spirit. Now we are destined to win, instead of our old state of being destined to lose.

I confess my belief that in Christ I now have a spiritual mind. Through faith I am now an overcomer of sin (and sinning). My faith is founded on the rock of God's Word of promise. In obedience to the Spirit of Christ, I, like Paul, keep my body under control in all things.

ROMANS 8:7

> Because the carnal [flesh-controlled] mind is enmity against God: for it is not subject to the law of God, neither indeed can be.

Paul is repeatedly teaching us what Adam should have kept before his eyes. Even the flesh that is free from the control of sin can desire things contrary to God's will for our lifestyle.

As a second Adam-man I rejoice that I am now walking in Christ's promise in John 8:34 and 36 that the Son sets us free from being slaves to sin and sinning. But I must remember that through doubt and temptations in my flesh, I can fall as Adam did. Jesus could have sinned too if He had accepted the temptations Satan offered to please His flesh instead of His Father. Adam was cast away by God, never to return to paradise because he was in the position described in Hebrews 10:26–29:

> For if we sin wilfully after that we have received the knowledge of the truth, there remaineth no more sacrifice for sins, But a certain fearful looking for of judgment and fiery indignation, which shall devour the adversaries. He that despised Moses' law died without mercy under two or three witnesses: Of how much sorer punishment, suppose ye, shall he be thought worthy, who hath trodden under foot the Son of God, and hath counted the blood of the covenant, wherewith he was sanctified, an unholy thing, and hath done despite unto the Spirit of grace?
>
> —HEBREWS 10:26–29

That scripture teaches us it is the unforgivable sin against the Holy Spirit for a Spirit-led man to fall back into willful sinning. It happened to Adam, and it can happen to me. My mind, by faith, must remain tuned to the Holy Spirit and not listen to any contrary demands of my flesh.

Romans 8:8

So then they that are in the flesh cannot please God.

Romans 8 is the why and the how of a sinless life in the Spirit. This is the life that Jesus came down from heaven to buy for us, to make us His spotless bride. The price was His life. Romans 5:10 states that we "shall be saved by His life."

Wait a minute, you may think. *I was already saved by His blood.* If you are using the word *saved* to mean "reconciled to God," you are correct. We are all reconciled—saved by Christ's shed blood.

But our future salvation from God's wrath at our judgment (our eternal life) depends entirely on the power of Christ's life—"the law of the Spirit of life in Christ Jesus," as Romans 8:1–2 promises—giving us a sinless, non-condemnable lifestyle while we are in our bodies of flesh. The kingdom of God, according to Romans 14:17, is "righteousness, and peace, and joy in the Holy Ghost." For a complete explanation of the doctrine of righteousness please read my book, *Go and Sin No More.*[1]

If the flesh is not subject to God's Spirit, it walks by sight and cannot please God. Faith, not sight, is the basic requirement if we are to please God.

If you see a man committing sin and do nothing to resist it, you are guilty with him. His blood will be upon his own head, but at whose hand will God require it? What does God say regarding a watchman?

> So you, son of man: I have made you a watchman for the house of Israel; therefore you shall hear a word from My mouth and warn them for Me. When I say to the wicked, "O wicked man, you shall surely die!" and you do not speak to warn the wicked from his way, that wicked man shall die in his iniquity; but his blood I will require at your hand."
>
> —Ezekiel 33:7–8

This is true of all men, if you allow a neighbor who is within reach of your influence to sin unwarned, he will die in his iniquity, but his blood will be required at your hand. If you keep silent, your silence encourages him in sin, or at least that you don't care about it—especially if he knows that you profess to be a Christian. Silence is consent. Sinners do regard your silence as approval for what they do.[2]

> And hereby we know that he abideth in us, by the Spirit which he hath given us.
>
> —1 John 3:24

Chapter 25

Am I a Christian?

Romans 8:9 says:

> But ye are not in the flesh, but in the Spirit, if so be that the Spirit of God dwell in you. Now if any man have not the Spirit of Christ, he is none of his.

In the Book of Acts, people had to have a personal Pentecost experience to know they had received the Spirit of Christ. The Bible teaches that the Spirit of Christ may also be called the Holy Spirit and the Spirit of the Father. He is the Spirit of God, and He is God. Acts records that Spirit baptism usually followed water baptism and was mostly imparted by the laying on of hands. But, as Acts 10:45 shows, it also happened before water baptism and without the laying-on of hands.

However, it was always evidenced by a manifestation. First John 3:9 says that the true sign of receiving and walking by the Spirit is that we will find that we now cannot sin. We will find ourselves to be new creations. Suddenly we cannot get Jesus out of our mind, and we will lose the desire to sin (the lusts of the flesh)!

Best-selling author Fritz Ridenour wrote: "Some Christians fail because they do not even know they have the Holy Spirit within them. But perhaps a lot more Christians fail because the concept of the Holy Spirit within is only that—a nice idea, a pat theological cliché that does not have a thing to do with their real lives."[1]

He continues: "But the Holy Spirit is not just a 'concept.' He is a Person. He is the Spirit of Christ and he does have something to do with your life, especially if you are interested in living a Christian life and not just being religious."

From my own experience and the testimony of hundreds to whom I have spoken, I can assure you that the reality of the Holy Spirit within immediately dispels the old idea of Him being a concept. His presence within you *immediately* changes you from being religious into being a Christian. The Holy Spirit does not just have *something* to do with our lives, but *everything*. Many who do not yet have the Holy Spirit consider themselves Christians. But Paul rightly points out that "if any man have not the Spirit of Christ, he is none of his" (Romans 8:9). Without the Holy Spirit, we are not really Christian at all.

Millions received the worldwide outpouring of the Holy Spirit in the last part of the twentieth century. They testified that they had been church-going "Christians" for many years, but they did not realize they had not been Christ's at all until they received the Spirit inside in a personal Pentecost.

From the instant we receive the gift of the Holy Spirit, our knowing Christ is moved from our head to our heart. It's such a short distance, but we could not do it. He did it.

We will then know without question, as Paul has been teaching us, that we are no longer the old, carnal man but a Spirit-man. In John 16:6–7, Jesus told His disciples not to be sad that He was returning to heaven. He explained that unless He did so, we would not be able to receive His Holy Spirit to comfort us with His love, guidance, gifts, and fruit.

Romans 8:10

> And if Christ be in you, the body is dead because of sin; but the Spirit is life because of righteousness.

In this verse, Paul draws a sharp difference between sin and righteousness. Nobody can be sinning and righteous at the same time. Christ took our bodies to death with Him, and we accepted our death by faith in His Word. However, because of sin, our bodies of flesh have yet to go to the grave, which awaits them at the cemetery.

As our corpse goes down into the earth, our spiritual self will go to irreversible eternal life because of our righteous lifestyle that brought life to our spirit from the Spirit of life in Christ Jesus. We overcome the power of sin by our faith-death with Christ. However, sin—although defeated and powerless—is still awaiting a chance to get back in, and it has to be finally given no more opportunity by our physical death. Or if the Lord comes back before we die, our flesh-and-blood body will be changed "in the twinkling of an eye" and we will find ourselves in a spiritual body (1 Cor. 15:50–53).

Flesh and blood cannot inherit the eternal kingdom of Jesus Christ. We cannot get to heaven in our natural body. That is why we should look on death as our doorway to paradise, but not if we decide to open that door ourselves by suicide.

Romans 8:11

> But if the Spirit of him that raised up Jesus from the dead dwell in you, he that raised up Christ from the dead shall also quicken your mortal bodies by his Spirit that dwelleth in you.

Christ's Spirit raised Him from the dead. His Spirit is also the Spirit of the Father. His Spirit is a person (He) whom the Bible calls the Holy Spirit and the Holy Ghost. He is the Spirit of God.

Therefore, we need to cherish and obey Christ's gift of His Spirit. If we do not obey Him, we grieve Him, and willful sin quenches Him. *To quench* means "to extinguish." But you may ask, "What about God's everlasting mercy?" Well, the Bible warns us that we can exclude ourselves from His mercy. Hebrews 12:14–17 says:

> Follow peace with all men, and holiness, without which no man shall see the Lord: Looking diligently lest any man fail of the grace of God...Lest there be any fornicator, or profane person, as Esau, who for one morsel of meat sold his birthright. For ye know how that afterward, when he would have inherited the blessing, he was rejected: for he found no place of repentance, though he sought it carefully with tears.

Dear Christian, listen to the words of Hebrews 6:4–6:

> For it is impossible for those who were once enlightened...and were made partakers of the Holy Ghost...If they shall fall away, to renew them again unto repentance; seeing they crucify to themselves the Son of God afresh, and put him to an open shame.

It was our sins that caused Jesus to be crucified. If you have watched the recent movie *The Passion of the Christ,* I am sure that you do not want your sin to do it afresh. No more forgiveness is available for a Christian who quenches the Spirit of Christ. We need His Spirit to resurrect us at His return. Christ first came for sinners, but His Second Coming is for those who are without sin. He will come for the sinless, righteous, and resurrected to join Him in the clouds for their promised inheritance of eternal salvation in His kingdom.

Romans 8:23 expresses our response to this blessed hope. It says that we who have the Holy Spirit "groan within ourselves, waiting for... the [eventual] redemption of our body." We are eagerly and expectantly hoping for that day of our eternal salvation. In Revelation 22:20, Jesus says, "Surely I come quickly." We cry, "Even so, *come, Lord Jesus.*"

Romans 8:12–13

> Therefore, brethren, we are debtors, not to the flesh, to live after the flesh. For if ye live after the flesh, ye shall die: but if ye through the Spirit do mortify the deeds of the body, ye shall live.

I have a body of flesh, a soul (my mind), and a spirit. My flesh is concerned with influencing my mind toward its own temporal desires and satisfaction. My flesh is not concerned with the unseen realm of God's kingdom. Indeed it is an enemy of that kingdom.

But now the Spirit of God lives in my spirit, and my mind, by faith, only listens to and obeys my spirit, which is one with the Holy Spirit. This is how I have the mind of Christ and not the carnal flesh-mind of the natural man. I abide in Christ's Spirit by faith, a faith that I possess as a gift from Him. I cannot work up faith by myself. As Ephesians 2:8 says, I receive faith by God's grace alone. I am very careful not to stand against and frustrate God's grace by looking again to the Law of commandments or religious laws for my righteous behavior.

Abiding by faith in the Spirit of life in Christ Jesus, I keep the mind of Christ and *obey* Him. In this way, I will not be tricked into allowing sin to regain control of my flesh and take me to the punishment of hellfire. The mind of Christ puts to death (mortifies) the wrong desires of my flesh. Therefore I am "dead indeed unto sin, but alive unto God through Jesus Christ our Lord," as promised in Romans 6:11.

ROMANS 8:14

> For as many as are led by the Spirit of God, they are the sons of God.

Am I being led by the Spirit of God? This can be a burning question in the mind of a Spirit-filled Christian. Only three things can stop us from walking in the Spirit:

- We have not been filled with the Spirit.
- We have quenched the Spirit by deliberate sinning.
- We are not believing and confessing that the Spirit of God is leading our every thought and action. We are in doubt!

Check yourself out! If you find that you are not leading a sinless lifestyle, it is certain that the Spirit of God is not leading you. We must be disobeying Him. We have reverted to obeying our flesh and can no longer look on ourselves as a child of God.

But if we are not a child of God, we will not be in line for our inheritance. Therefore, it is time to change!

Start walking by faith in God's promises, which we have outlined in Romans 6–8. Nobody else can do this for you. We all have the same option that Eve originally possessed. We can walk by faith and obey Christ's promises or else we can walk in doubt and obey our own flesh. The end is either eternal life or eternal death. Man is either righteous, or he is a sinner. Satan and his world system are out to trick us into making the wrong decision.

You, like me, may be believing and confessing from your heart that your old man is dead—that it is not you who lives in your flesh but Christ who lives in you. Then you will find that you are walking righteously, free from sinning and in obedience to His promise. You will know that you are a Son of God. Sons of God are brothers of Jesus!

We, as sons of God, are not on a merry-go-round of sin-and-repent each week. Merry-go-rounds have wonderful music, but they leave us where we started. Satan will be waiting for us at the same place we got on.

Romans 8:15

> For ye have not received the spirit of bondage again to fear; but ye have received the Spirit of adoption, whereby we cry, Abba, Father.

I believe that the spirit of bondage is the Law given on tablets of stone to Moses. This is shown in Galatians 2:4 and Romans 7:14. The Law gave power to sin, which leads to death as 2 Corinthians 3:6 explains when it says, "The letter killeth, but the spirit giveth life."

Since Pentecost, we are able to live by the Spirit of Christ. In Christ, we are adopted as sons by His Father and our Father. Now, by His Spirit, our Father pours His peace and love into our hearts, as shown in Ephesians 6:23. God's "perfect love casteth out fear" (1 John 4:18).

When I meet people who have received the Spirit in His recent downloading over the last fifty-odd years, they all bear witness to the change of lifestyle that overtakes them when God's love suddenly overpowers their hearts. I can bear witness to it myself! My Bible belief that God is love became a personal experience. In the words of Song of Solomon 5:8, I became "sick of love [lovesick]."

Song of Solomon 4:10 says that God's love is better than wine. I often find his love more intoxicating than strong drink used to be for me. As Song of Solomon 8:7 declares, "Many waters cannot quench [His] love...if a man would give for love all the wealth of his house, it would be utterly despised."

God, by His love, assures me that He is my eternal Father. His love makes it easy for me to obey Him. I cannot bear the thought of offending Him. I am resolved to never give up my adoption by returning to the Law and its curses.

A man does not live conscientiously toward God or man unless he is in the habit of reproving transgressors within his influence. This is one reason that there is so little conscience in the church today. No man can have a clear conscience who sees sin and does not reprove it. Just speak the truth out of love!

> ...let us lay aside every weight, and the sin which doth so easily beset us, and let us run with patience the race that is set before us.
>
> —Hebrews 12:1

Chapter 26

WHY SUFFERING?

ROMANS 8:16–17 SAYS:

> The Spirit itself beareth witness with our spirit, that we are the children of God: And if children, then heirs; heirs of God, and joint-heirs with Christ; if so be that we suffer with him, that we may be also glorified together.

It is through a person, Christ's Spirit, that we become adopted as sons of God. We experience our adoption as children by the love and kindness our Father pours into our hearts each day by His Spirit. Admittedly we feel it more some days than others.

But love and kindness touch our emotions, and emotions are

subject to fluctuations too. Whether it is love or tears, I can be sure that the Holy Spirit does not let me get into a settled rut. Life as a child of God is never boring. In fact, it is better described as *thrilling*. I soon recognize that I am only a child. Most things I do on my own are failures, and I soon learn to act only in accordance with my Father's will, as His Spirit directs me.

If I revert to doing my own thing, Proverbs 16:18 becomes a reality for me. It simply states: "Pride goeth before destruction, and an haughty spirit before a fall."

It is right that I should feel proud of the privilege of being chosen as a child of God with a promised inheritance of eternal life in His kingdom. But I must never lose sight of the fact that my carelessness can cut me out of that inheritance. Hebrews 12:16–17 tells how Esau lost his inheritance, though he sought it with tears.

Paul is a good example for us. He did not become proud or presumptuous when God poured His power into his earthen vessel to show—as he called it—"that the excellency of the power may be of God, and not of us" (2 Cor 4:7). Rather, in 2 Corinthians 12:10, he rejoices in his weakness, "for when I am weak, then am I strong." Being weak as a child leads me to be dependent on and obedient to my "Abba, Father" (Rom. 8:15).

I do not forget that I am a brother and joint heir with Christ, for without Him I am a nobody. And just as Christ suffered as the firstborn Son, I am required to share in that suffering. For Paul, writing in 2 Corinthians 11:24–33 and Galatians 6:17, suffering meant whippings, shipwreck, jail, and the marks in his body of the crucified Christ, not to mention false brothers and being stoned to apparent death.

Suffering always comes from the hand of God, our loving Father. It comes to prepare us to be worthy to share in the inheritance of our firstborn Brother, Jesus, who Himself was made "perfect through sufferings" (Heb. 2:10).

First Peter 4:12–13 discusses suffering, and says that we should not think it "strange concerning the fiery trial which is to try you" as we "are partakers of Christ's sufferings; that, when his glory shall be revealed, ye may be glad also with exceeding joy." The Book of Job and many other Old Testament verses and New Testament scriptures tell about people who had more than a fair share of suffering.

We, like Jesus in Gethsemane, may cry out to our Father, "If it be possible, let this cup [of suffering] pass from me" (Matt. 26:39). But one way or another, it has to be borne if we are to obtain our promised inheritance in glory.

A long time ago, Mrs. Job was complaining about the bad treatment that God had allowed Satan to put on her and her husband. Job, our example, cried out to his wife, "What? shall we receive good at the hand of God, and shall we not receive evil?" (Job 2:10).

It is now well known that underground churchmen in China consider it a great honor to suffer as their brothers Jesus, Paul, and all the great saints. When I was in China, I noticed that their faces take on a special glow when they discuss their jail terms, some for twenty years or more.

Paul exhorts us in Romans 12:1 to "present your bodies a living sacrifice, holy, acceptable unto God, which is your reasonable service." We get an opportunity to do this whenever sickness strikes our bodies.

Romans 8:17 concludes with the promise that the end of suffering is to be glorified together with Jesus. What a contrast to the perspective of the world, which looks on suffering as an enemy to be avoided and overcome at all costs, an enemy that leads to death. But we who are in Christ Jesus recognize suffering as a friend that leads us to glorification with Jesus.

Would the great joy of springtime be breathtaking if winter had not first come? The joy of the Spirit was born out of the cross. We, like Jesus, are called to suffer in silence when our brothers and sisters bring disgrace on the church and on Christ or condemn us unjustly. They are part of His family—our family.

We must beware of their leaven and defend the truth; we must treat them as brothers, yet not eat with them. God is their Father too, and He will do the chastising and, if necessary, take revenge. They are the tares and the useless fish that He will discard on the last day. Unless they are directly under our authority, we must leave them to the Lord. Otherwise, God's purpose cannot be worked in them or in us.

By obeying the Spirit we will learn how to suffer all forms of abuse and unjust persecution from our brothers and from anyone in authority over us. Reading about the lives of Jesus, His disciples, and people in the early church will aid us in understanding how to treat "black-sheep" brothers. We should also read about the lives of the outstanding saints down through the centuries.

Romans 8:18

> For I reckon that the sufferings of this present time are not worthy to be compared with the glory which shall be revealed in us.

Paul is using the word *reckon* in the bookkeeper's sense. It means, "I have irrefutable evidence." Paul would have experienced this irrefutable evidence when he was transported to heaven, an experience he describes in 2 Corinthians 12:2–10. He knew that a true Christian who is living righteously is going to experience not only the sufferings common to all mankind, but also the sufferings of persecution that come from both outside and inside the church. Therefore, in his kindly manner, he softens the blows by impressing on us that the sufferings—no matter how bad—are nothing in comparison with the glory laid up for the one who suffers.

Jesus, our brother, set His face as flint, determined to go up to Jerusalem for the last time, knowing that He was heading for the terrible sufferings which the prophets had foretold awaited Him. In Luke 24:26, He told His traveling companions on the road to Emmaus that He did it for the glory that was set before Him.

> But let judgment run down as waters, and righteousness as a mighty stream.
>
> —Amos 6:24

Chapter 27

Glory Awaits Us!

If we are in a lifestyle of living the law of the Spirit of life in Christ Jesus; we are free from sinning and therefore under no possible condemnation. We are also certain that glory awaits us.

Sadly, most Christians seem to think that they are sinning if they are not perfect in all the virtues. I often hear them scoffing that nobody is perfect, and therefore everybody sins (even if it is just a little). The gospel truth is that being righteous and being perfect are two separate things.

Christians are empowered by the Spirit and expected by our Father to walk sinlessly from day one of being born of the Spirit. From that day onward, the Spirit starts to work on sanctifying and perfecting our virtues. An immature tree that produces its first crop of fruit cannot expect the fruit to be perfect. Perfect fruit will be the result of age, pruning, summers and hard winters, dry times, and times of watering.

We cannot have our fruit of the Spirit brought to perfection while we are still under bondage to sin and sinning. Christ took us to death to free us from sin and the Law of Commandments so that He could then go on and perfect us by the ongoing work of His Spirit. This fact is explained in John 12:24, where He said, "Except a corn of wheat fall into the ground and die, it abideth alone: but if it die, it bringeth forth much fruit." In Matthew 13:8, Jesus told about seed that "fell into good ground, and brought forth fruit, some an hundredfold, some sixtyfold, some thirtyfold."

In thirty years of closely studying the doctrines of the Christian churches, I have found, to my sorrow, that most of the teachings in the church today are bound by man-taught tradition. They declare that because we are not perfect at conversion, we cannot walk sinless from that day forward.

I repeat the truth that our study of Romans 6–8 has so far revealed. Sinlessness is a gift of God—His grace—given at true conversion. It is a prerequisite for being taken by the Spirit (God's grace) on to perfecting the virtues of the fruit of the Holy Spirit (the Spirit of Jesus and His Father). This perfecting is only hindered by our resistance to change and our general unwillingness to be completely detached from the possessions of this world. The flesh clings to possessions, including worldly family, relations, and friends.

Being perfected is not so much a matter of time, but of accepting the spiritual world of God and rejecting the fleshly things of this transient world. In Luke 18:18–25, Jesus told the young man who came asking for perfection, "I am glad that you walk without sinning against the written Law of God. But if you want to be perfect, you must forsake all your possessions and follow me." Notice that Jesus separated sinlessness from perfection. Once Jesus saw that this rich young idealist already was walking sinlessly as far as the law was concerned,

He was prepared to instruct him about the way of perfection. On another occasion, Jesus said unless you forsake everything you cannot be my disciples. How many can claim to be disciples of Jesus today?

Dear Reader, do not despair, but allow the indwelling Spirit to lead you to the level of perfection God has predestined for you. He will call you to be detached from possessions. He has called you to holiness, without which no man will see God (Heb. 12:14). I believe that our level of perfection will determine our rank in heaven!

In the following verse, the author of Hebrews is saying, "Keep your eyes on your future, not on any suffering in this life!"

> For they [our earthly fathers] verily for a few days chastened us after their own pleasure; but he [our Father] for our profit, that we might be partakers of his holiness.
>
> —Hebrews 12:10

The rest of the letter to the Romans is beyond the scope of this book and generally describes the path to perfection. This path is available for the believer who is already set free from sinning by faith in Christ's promises. Dear Reader, that is now you.

> I proclaim righteousness in the great assembly; I do not seal my lips, as you know, O Lord. I do not hide your righteousness in my heart; I speak of your faithfulness and salvation. I do not conceal your love and your truth from the great assembly.
>
> —Psalm 40:9–10, NIV

Part III

Visions, Words, and Healing

Chapter 28

VISIONS, WORDS, AND DREAMS!

ACTS 10:17, 19 says:

> Now while Peter doubted in himself what this vision which he had seen should mean...the Spirit said unto him, Behold, three men seek thee.

I can never forget my first vision from heaven. During the month of August, the Coral Sea lapped the golden sands of Kurrimine Beach to the tune of "tat, tat, tat, tat," a distinct rhythm made by the rippling fronds of the coconut palms that line the foreshore. Dunk Island sat shimmering on the horizon like a romantic Bali Hai, and the shallow water over the coral reef and the sandbars reflected a variety of soft colors. For those on holiday, the balmy spring days enticed them to take a nap after lunch.

The children were playing on the beach a few yards from our cottage door, and my wife was sewing on the front deck as I stretched myself out on the bed, ready to relax and drift off. The moment I shut my eyes, I saw the face of a man in a vision as bright as a picture on a color television screen. He appeared to be only about three feet away, and he did not move, but looked at me intently. Having a rounded face, fair skin, blue eyes, and aged about forty, he reminded me of the paintings of Caesar I had seen at school.

He was certainly not anyone I knew. Wondering what on earth was happening, I opened my eyes for a few moments to make sure I was not asleep. As soon as I shut my eyes again, the same bright face was looking at me. I was amazed and a bit shocked, so I kept opening and closing my eyes until I was positive that I was not dreaming or imagining things. Finally I took an intense look and saw that his face had a couple of really large warts on one cheek. After a few minutes, the vision disappeared, and I lay there thinking, *Lord, what is all this about?*

But nothing unusual happened until the next day. Once more, when I shut my eyes at siesta time, the same bright face appeared. Again amazed, I went through the opening and closing of my eyes to test the whole thing over and over, to be sure I was not dreaming. I really knew I was not because the face was far too bright for a dream or an imagination. But I had no explanation.

Of course, the next day, as I lay down after lunch, I was looking forward to seeing the vision again. But there was nothing. I thought, *In Your time, Lord,* and soon drifted off to the "tat, tat, tat" of the palm fronds dancing in rhythm with the caressing breeze. As I drifted off, I saw a sea eagle gliding by with a whiting clutched in his claws. Startled, I awoke from a vivid dream when my son, Mark, shook me and said, "Wake up Dad. Roy Dickson is on the phone."

I had been dreaming that a man was leading me to the back of the Innisfail Assembly of God church, a place I had never been in my life. This man kept telling me that he wanted to introduce me to a person named Bernie Gray. But just as he said, "Here is Bernie Gray," my son woke me up. All I had seen of Bernie was his hand.

Roy Dickson was the local mayor at that time. I thought, *He is phoning me about an engineering project I'm working on,* and I was all set to tell him "Sorry, Roy, but I'm on holidays."

However, the first words he spoke shook me to my roots. "Hello Geoff, I want you to come to a church in our town of Innisfail at ten o'clock tomorrow morning to meet a man called Bernie Gray."

Before I dropped the phone with shock, I managed to say, "I'll be there for sure, Roy." Roy had gathered six other men at the church the next day. As we sat waiting for Bernie Gray to arrive, I was musing to myself about whether or not his face would be the one I had been given in the visions. But I told none of the men about it. *Who was this Bernie Gray? Why was he coming?*

When he walked in, his face was the one I had seen in my visions at the beach. *But how could I be sure?* I could see no warts on his cheek—*but hold on*! As he turned his face to the light, there they were, almost indiscernible. I found out later that he was born with them. They were a type of birthmark. I realized that the Lord had showed this mark to me in an enlarged version so there would be no mistake that Bernie Gray was the face in the visions.

The moment Bernie said, "I am the Australian Director of the Full Gospel Businessmen's (FGB) Fellowship," my heart leaped within me. When he called for men to form a chapter in Innisfail, mine was the first hand to go up.

That night I thought of how Peter the Apostle had been given a vision to prepare him to go to the house of the non-Jew Cornelius. I then realized that the Lord had set me to be a part of FGB. I opened my Bible and read, "For we are his workmanship, created in Christ Jesus unto good works, which God hath before ordained that we should walk in them." (Eph. 2:10).

We had over 160 people at our first dinner, and we saw Pentecost all over again! Through the FGB functions and prayer meetings, a Holy Ghost revival shook the district, and He crossed all the denominational fences in a stride.

The existing Pentecostal church had to buy a larger church building. Another Pentecostal church was soon opened to take care of all those who were being set on fire by the Holy Spirit.

Jesus had prepared me for this sovereign move by baptizing me with the His Spirit while I was praying in my bedroom two years before. The revival saw my wife and seven grown children swept along by the Spirit into the kingdom of Jesus Christ. Now we have grandchildren walking in the Spirit and serving in His realm. I believe this book would not have been written without that vision from the Lord, Roy Dickson's obedience, and Bernie Gray's leadership.

I have found that a vision from the Lord bears good fruit. It cannot be turned on or off by self. It is exceptionally bright, and it cannot be erased from the memory. A vision is completely different from a dream. Even though the eyes are usually closed in a vision, one is still awake.

We do not need to have visions or dreams nor hear His voice to walk in obedience to his Spirit. However, I suggest that we should always expect them.

Perhaps it is because I am slow at picking things up, but the Spirit of God often has spoken to me in a voice that, though it comes from outside, cannot be heard by others around me. Hearing Him speak is not the same as a prophetic utterance, which can come out of one's mouth without thinking.

Chapter 29

His Book and Around the World

Isaiah 50:5 says:

> The Lord God hath opened mine ear, and I was not rebellious.

The first time I heard God's voice was in the early hours of the morning. He woke me up with a whisper and said, "Every word in My Book is a prayer." I was intrigued that He spoke of the Bible as "My Book." He was telling me to read His Word slowly, to chew every word thoroughly before swallowing and digesting it.

Later I learned that reading or listening to God's Word being preached is like eating a meat pie (my favorite meal). If we strike a piece of gristle as we chew, we stop munching, take it out of our mouth, and put it in the garbage. I pass on to you what the Lord said that morning, knowing that it will revolutionize your Bible reading as it did mine. It took me a few years to tie Christ's words into Luke 4:4, where He said, "Man shall not live by bread alone, but by every word of God."

One day, while I was standing alone on the tarmac of the Sydney airport, I heard a voice from behind me say with some authority, "Go and see My world." I turned to see who was speaking with such authority, but there was no one to be seen. Later, as I pondered over these words, I was again intrigued that He used the word *My* to describe what He had created.

Financially and businesswise, it was impossible for me to do it. But I said to Him, "Lord, if these words are from You, then *You* will have to arrange the finances and the opportunity." I was putting out a fleece.

I thought little more about it, but at the end of twelve months, I was stunned to find that I was all set to go and see God's world. It developed because of increased business income and a need to look at overseas projects. I even had sufficient funds to take my wife with me as my secretary.

We purchased round-the-world tickets with Pan Am Airways, which took us from Sydney, Australia, to Honolulu to Tokyo to Manila to Hong Kong to Singapore to Bombay to Frankfurt. From Frankfurt we took the train to Hamburg to Holland to Paris to Spain to the Riviera to Rome. Then we traveled by plane again to Cairo and across the Sinai to Jerusalem to Athens. We went by train again to Thessalonica and through then-Yugoslavia, stopping at the island of Hvar and the interior city of Titograd. Back in the air, we flew to Zurich and the Alps and on to London.

We toured the British Isles by car, flew to Ireland, and then on to Kenya and South Africa, on to New York, and up to Detroit for the world convention of FGB, where fifteen thousand had gathered at the Renaissance Centre. Then it was on to Miami, Panama, Rio, and Argentina, finally returning home via Jackson City, Los Angeles, Las Vegas, Salt Lake City, and San Francisco.

It took three months. We rarely booked ahead, but relied on God to guide us where to lodge each night. I had obeyed His command to see His world, and I had seen all the projects regarding my own business. I had given my testimony at FGB meetings in nearly every country we visited, and I still had a few dollars in my pocket. We were both aged 56 and had, until then, never been outside of Australia except to Nauru and New Guinea.

I mention this trip around God's world to show that He prepares His Spirit-filled people in various ways and equips them to do the good works he has prepared for them before the foundation of His world. Back home, I began to see the world from God's perspective. He sees the whole of His creation, first globally, then nationally, then families, then individuals, and finally His own worldwide body, the church.

As we visited the churches in each nation, we were struck with the way we heard prayers offered for their own country but rarely for the body of Christ throughout the world. We came home with a new frame of mind based on firsthand experience. We no longer see the church as having different skin colors and faces or different cultures or languages. Instead we see it purely as brothers and sisters in His Spirit and each a member of His body. God did give me a special affinity with the people of Japan.

I did not know then that God was preparing me to preach, teach, and write books to His church, calling for a reformation. We, the church of the last days, have His joy in the Spirit and His peace in the Spirit. But as yet, we are not walking in righteousness. We should know that "the kingdom of God is... righteousness, and peace, and joy in the Holy Ghost" (Rom. 14:17).

We have a mind-set that Satan has foisted on us—that we

are sinners until the day we die. But the new covenant says that we are "a royal priesthood" (1 Pet. 2:9). We are a special people who were once the slaves of sin but now have been freed from slavery to sin (according to John 8:34, 36). We have become slaves of righteousness (as seen in Romans 6:18), for anyone born of God "cannot sin" (1 John 3:9). I have been commissioned to repeat Paul's warning, "Wake up, church! Stop sinning before it is too late."

I am convinced that Satan will tolerate preachers who teach doctrines about salvation, as long as they do not preach that sin, for the individual, has been defeated. Since sin has been overcome, it follows that without holiness (righteousness), no man will see God.

Holy, righteous men will one day see God because they walk sinlessly by faith in Jesus Christ through "the law of the Spirit of life" (Rom. 8:2). In the eighteenth century, the Wesley brothers taught the reality of the sinless walk, and England underwent a spontaneous revival. Charles Finney taught the sinless walk in the nineteenth century and fired a revival across North America. At that time of Civil War, the nation was hungry for righteousness. Out of Finney's teaching and his Oberlin College came the Pentecostal revival of the twentieth century, a revival that has touched churches globally.

This revival, in which we are still living, is pointing us to return to the way of righteousness and reformation. But are we hungry for righteousness? Jesus says that only those who "hunger and thirst after righteousness" will be filled (Matt. 5:6).

Dear Reader, are you hungry for the sinless walk of righteousness? Does it consume you? Or are you living in the daydream that you are already guaranteed a place in heaven whether you continue sinning or not. I appeal: It's time to wake up, church! And that is Bible.

The streets of Detroit were crowded with pedestrians hurrying home from work. As I scurried across the busy street on the green light, the Lord spoke to me in a loud voice that no one else seemed to hear. He said, "You are a king and a priest."

I needed to hear that. I was returning from a meeting where the preacher had been insisting that I would surely go on sinning until my death. I knew that the preacher was wrong, but he was well-respected internationally, and I was a nobody in church circles. *Perhaps I was wrong after all.*

But the Holy Spirit's words to me on that busy street cleared the air. Kings and priests in the kingdom of Jesus Christ are not poor old sinners in slavery to sin. That night I read from the New Testament that Jesus Christ washed me from my past sins in His own blood and has made me a king and a priest to His Father. To Him be glory and dominion for ever and ever. My dictionary reveals that a king is a preeminent person and a priest is one set apart, acceptable to God to offer Him sacrifices.

I found that I belong to "a chosen generation, a royal priesthood, an holy nation, a peculiar [special] people; that... [God] hath called... out of darkness into his marvelous light [of righteousness]" (1 Pet. 2:9). I am no longer a sinner who was reconciled to God by grace. I have become a son of God led by His Spirit in all goodness, righteousness, and truth. Persevering in this walk in the Spirit will assure me of the inheritance that my heavenly Father has prepared for those of us who do righteously.

What a thrill and a comfort it became to know that I am a king and a priest in His kingdom! I believe it!

Chapter 30

How I Was Completely Healed of Asthma

Luke 5:17 says:

> ...and the power of the Lord was present to heal them.

In 1975, the disease that was taking me to an early grave had forced me to my knees. And it was on my knees, after 180 days of bedtime prayers, that Jesus filled me with His Spirit. A week after I received the baptism in the Holy Spirit, I was a passenger in my friend Eddie's car. It was late at night. The headlight beams were lighting up a mountain pass as he skillfully eased us through the sharp, hairpin curves. All was quiet.

Suddenly the authoritative voice of the Spirit spoke to me. He said, "You have been healed of your disease of asthma, and you will never get it again. I cured you on the night I came to your bedroom and filled you with My presence." They were the sweetest words I had ever heard, and of course they turned out to be true. That was twenty-nine years ago, and my wife, Margaret, can testify that I have never had another asthma attack since the night the Holy Spirit came.

He did not tell me that He had also healed me of the disease of sin, which was taking me to spiritual death. I knew in my heart that He had, but He wanted me to wait to discover it for myself in His Word and then walk in it by faith. This book you are reading, together with my earlier book *Go and Sin No More,* is the result of that discovery. His Spirit brings life—abundant life. The letter of the Law brings death.

Chapter 31

Take Your Glory, Lord

Luke 6:38 says:

> Give, and it shall be given unto you; good measure, pressed down, and shaken together, and running over, shall men give into your bosom. For with the same measure that ye mete withal it shall be measured to you again.

I believe you will be encouraged to learn of a man I know. In obedience to the Spirit, he has, at various times, given away just over one hundred thousand dollars to those in need. In return, God has given him, at various times, over two hundred thousand dollars. It came to him as gifts from men who knew nothing of his alms. He did not have to work for it. It came as gifts.

This is Christ's faithfulness to fulfill His promise that we reap what we sow:

> But this I say, He which soweth sparingly shall reap also sparingly; and he which soweth bountifully shall reap also bountifully. Every man according as he purposeth in his heart, so let him give; not grudgingly, or of necessity: for God loveth a cheerful giver. And God is able to make all grace abound toward you; that ye, always having all sufficiency in all things, may abound to every good work:(As it is written, He hath dispersed abroad; he hath given to the poor: his righteousness remaineth for ever.
>
> —2 Corinthians 9:6–9

Jesus said, too, that it is wise to make friends by using "the mammon [money] of unrighteousness" (Luke 16:9).

It may be helpful for you to know that since the day of my personal Pentecost, I have not been in the red at my bank. Nor have I been to a doctor or chemist. I have not taken any painkillers or pills of any description. I trust Jesus alone. He is my everything!

Even though I have been indisposed several times, I use it to discover His will for me by simply offering my body (sick or well) as a living sacrifice and rest in the truth that He bore my sickness and carried my pain, as Matthew 8:16–17 says. He heals me every time—in His time! I find that stepping out in faith draws me closer to Him. I do not believe that I will never die, for there is a sickness unto death—unless He comes again before I leave my body.

Dear Reader, I leave you with a mighty promise of Jesus to His people:

> My sheep hear my voice, and I know them, and they follow me [in obedience]: And I give unto them eternal life; and they shall never perish, neither shall any man pluck them out of my hand.
>
> —John 10:27–28

The person whose lifestyle conforms to Luke 10:25 cannot sin and is therefore righteous in God's eyes. But to live that lifestyle, we need to walk in the Spirit of life (Rom. 8:1–12). We need to walk as born-of-God persons (with God as our Father) day-by-day by faith in Jesus Christ (1 John 3:9–10). You discover that your father is no longer God if you commit a sin, for then Satan is your father (1 John 3:8). Beware of the leaven of those who teach that you cannot lose your sonship with God and your inheritance, or that once reconciled always reconciled. Beware of those who teach that God forgives you every time you repent (Heb. 10).

Many are called but few are chosen, because of sins. The unrighteous cannot inherit the kingdom of God (1 Cor. 6:9; 2 Pet. 2:13). Beware of those who misunderstand the word *reward*. The souls in the lake of fire are still loved by God but it is too late for Him to save them from their eternal spiritual death.

Until we meet, I bless you in Jesus' name! Amen.

Epilogue

Writing to believers in Corinth, Paul said that we work at being accepted. For at our judgment, we will either be accepted or rejected. On that day, Jesus Christ our righteous judge will hand down His just decision that we are either acceptable to enter the eternal kingdom of heaven or that we are rejected with the word "Depart from Me, you cursed." Paul says that we work at avoiding the terror of our judge who sends the unacceptable Christians to the lake of fire with Satan forever and ever. We will be judges according to our works that we did in our bodies while on earth. If our works have been good, we will be accepted. If our works have been bad, we will be unacceptable!

The New Testament undeniably teaches everywhere that we will be judged not on faith, but on our works we have done after being born of God. Therefore, none can have a blessed assurance of being accepted on that day unless their works have been good. Paul says to work at it so you will be found to be living a blameless lifestyle on that day (2 Cor. 2:9–11; 1 Pet. 1:17; Matt. 25:31–46; Heb. 12:14, 17; 1 Cor. 1:8).

NOTES

Chapter 3
Stop Dreaming—Wake Up to Reality

1. Charles Spurgeon, "March 11 A.M.," *Morning and Evening* (Peabody, MA: Henrickson Publishers, 1991).

Chapter 5
God's Goodness and His Severity

1. *The Life of Teresa of Jesus* (New York: Doubleday, 1991), 217.
2. Howard F. Vos, *Nelson's Quick Reference: Introduction to Church History,* 4th edition (1994), 203.
3. Dr. and Mrs. Howard Taylor, Hudson Taylor, *The Growth of a Work of God* (Singapore: Overseas Missionary Fellowship, 1988).

Chapter 8
A Reformation of Righteousness through Love

1. Geoffrey Higham, *Go and Sin No More* (Lake Mary, FL: Creation House, 2004).
2. Grahame C. Martin, *Headhunters* (Sydney, Australia: Anzea Books, 1982).

Chapter 9
Fear God?

1. This is an excerpt from a three-part audio series entitled "Hebrew Spirituality" by Dwight A. Pryor (available at www.jcstudies.com). Used by permission of the author.
2. Ibid.

Chapter 11
Life After Death

1. Charles Finney, *Experiencing the Presence of God* (Springdale, PA: Whitaker House, 2000), 195.

Chapter 15
Conditions Do Apply

1. Saint Teresa of Avila, *The Life of Saint Teresa of Avila by Herself* (New York: Penguin Classics, 1957), 129. Translated by J.M. Cohen.

Chapter 16
Proud Humility

1. Finney, *Experiencing the Presence of God,* 488.

Chapter 18
Two Tigers

1. Saint Teresa of Avila, *The Life of Saint Teresa of Avila by Herself,* 306.
2. Finney, *Experiencing the Presence of God,* 493.

Chapter 22
Race to Win

1. Frank Peretti, *The Oath* (Nashville, TN: W Publishing Group, 1995).

Chapter 24
Not Condemned—Why Not?

1. Geoffrey Higham, *Go and Sin No More.*
2. Finney, *Experiencing the Presence of God,* 504.

Chapter 25
Am I a Christian?

1. Fritz Ridenour, *How to be a Christian Without Being Religious* (Ventura, CA: Regal Books, 2002).

Chapter 29
His Book and Around the World

1. Howard F. Vos, *Introduction to Church History* (Nashville, TN: Thomas Nelson, 1994), 234–235.

To Contact the Author

A large number of live weekly teachings on DVD and weekly one-page teachings on how to walk in holy righteousness are available by contacting:

Geoffrey Higham Ministries
85 Mourilyan Road
Innisfail 4860, Australia

Phone: national 07-40611326; international 61-740611326

E-mail: ghigham@dodo.com.au

Or

Innisfail House Church
M/S 1800
Mourilyan 4858, Australia

E-mail: JoeandLouise@aapt.net.au

Please become a part of this restoration!